# Dragonflies and Damselflies of Hertfordshire

# Dragonflies and Damselflies of Hertfordshire

Alan Reynolds
Revd Tom Gladwin
Christine Shepperson

ISBN: 978-0-9521685-6-0

First published in 2008 by the Hertfordshire Natural History Society

Hertfordshire Natural History Society
24 Mandeville Rise, Welwyn Garden City, Hertfordshire AL8 7JU
Registered Charity number 218418
www.hnhs.org

Published with generous assistance from
Environment Agency
Hertfordshire Dragonfly Group
Lee Valley Regional Park Authority
Herts and Middlesex Wildlife Trust

Designed by LTD Design Consultants, London SW1V 2AJ

Printed in Great Britain by Crowes Complete Print, Norwich, NR6 6JB

A catalogue record for this book is available from the British Library

# Foreword

Dragonflies are the ideal environmental barometer. By recording and estimating their numbers one can assess the status and quality of our aquatic habitats. As a general rule, the greater the number and diversity of dragonfly species at a site the better the quality of the aquatic environment in which they live.

Being brightly coloured and very noticeable in their behaviour they lend themselves to observation and study by naturalists and general public alike. Their aerial abilities are without equal in the insect world. There are skimmers, darters, chasers and hawkers, each name reflecting their mode of flight. Demoiselles and emeralds bear witness to their great beauty and attraction. One only has to take a summer walk near still or running freshwater to be aware of their presence and be drawn into further observation.

Hertfordshire has a long history of natural history recording and study by renowned naturalists. Over the years a number of county entomologists have reported their sightings in the local transactions, but there has never been an organised survey of the county's dragonfly fauna. This Atlas rectifies the situation, by bringing together previous knowledge in the county with the increased interest in dragonflies today.

The three authors have done a stupendous job to mobilise more than 100 recorders over a six-year period, to submit more than 14,000 records. This is no mean feat and is indicative of the drive and motivation they have brought to this Atlas Project. This Atlas provides a snapshot, which will stand the test of time, by providing a benchmark on which to judge future trends and changes in dragonfly distribution. This has never been more relevant as it is today with current concern over climate change. The authors can be justifiably proud of their contribution to Hertfordshire's Natural History.

**Steve Cham**
National Co-ordinator
British Dragonfly Society
(Dragonfly Recording Network)
Silsoe
Bedfordshire
December 2007

This book is dedicated to Hertfordshire's dragonfly recorders who carried out the fieldwork and without whom this book would not have been possible.

Hertfordshire Natural History Society promotes the study and recording of the county's flora and fauna and encourages a wider interest in natural history including the conservation of wildlife, habitats and geological features.

Established in 1875, the Society publishes the *Hertfordshire Bird Report* and *The Hertfordshire Naturalist* each year as part of the *Transactions of the Hertfordshire Natural History Society*, which have been documenting the changing face of the county for the last 130 years.

Other HNHS publications include:

*The Moths of Hertfordshire* by Colin Plant, 2008, ISBN 978-0-9521685-7-7

*The Mammals, Amphibians and Reptiles of Hertfordshire* by Michael Clark, 2001, ISBN 1-84019-012-4

*Birds at Tring Reservoirs* by Rob Young, Jack Fearnside and David Russell, 1996, ISBN 0-9521685-1-0

*The Breeding Birds of Hertfordshire* by K W Smith, C W Dee, J D Fearnside, E W Fletcher and R N Smith, 1993, ISBN 0-9521685-0-2

Further details from www.hnhs.org

*HNHS is registered charity number 218418*

# List of contents

# 1. Introduction and acknowledgements

Who can fail to be enthralled by the colourful spectacle and breathtaking aerodynamic agility of dragonflies as they cavort around reed-lined streams and ponds on warm summer days? These enigmatic creatures have always held a special place in our hearts, but most of us admit to knowing very little about them.

Fortunately, interest in these fantastic insects is on the increase, due partly to the recent publication of a selection of dragonfly field guides, but also due to a number of birdwatchers turning their attentions to these winged insects during the summer months, when birds settle down for the breeding season.

There are only 19 species of dragonfly regularly recorded in Hertfordshire and therefore, with the help of a pair of binoculars and one of the new field guides, it does not take long to start identifying the various species. So, on the next warm summers day, why not take a walk in the countryside next to a pond, lake, ditch or stream and start to enjoy these incredible creatures at close quarters.

Dragonfly recording today is a well-regulated process supported by an army of recorders equipped with high performance optics and comprehensive identification guides. Their records are submitted to county recorders who validate the records before adding them to a computer-controlled database. How different it must have been in days gone by.

The first published records of dragonflies in Hertfordshire were by James Francis Stephens in 1835. In his *Illustrations of British Entomology; or a Synopsis of Indigenous Insects, Vol VI* Stephens listed just four species of dragonfly (*Anisoptera*), Emperor Dragonfly *Anax imperator*, Brown Hawker *Aeshna grandis*, Migrant Hawker *Aeshna mixta* and Hairy Dragonfly *Brachytron pratense* as being found in Hertfordshire. Surprisingly no species of damselfly (*Zygoptera*) were included.

Throughout the remainder of the 19th century a number of other authors referred to Stephens' work, although no further species were added to the county list. Little attention seems to have been paid to the collection and study of dragonflies over this period, possibly due to the difficulty in preserving the colours of specimens. However, the publication of W Harcourt Bath's *Illustrated Handbook of British Dragonflies* (1890) would appear to have stimulated interest in the lead up to the 20th century.

In 1910 and 1911 E R Speyer published articles in *The Entomologist* listing 12 species of dragonfly recorded in Hertfordshire. These were the first county records, mainly from 1908, for which detailed information such as date, location and abundance was provided. Interestingly, Speyer omitted two species that had appeared in Stephens' list published some 75 years earlier.

During the first half of the 20th century, E R Speyer, A E Gibbs, D G Sevastopoulo, Ray Palmer, and Bertram and Sylvia Lloyd published papers on dragonflies observed in Hertfordshire. During this period there was correspondence between county entomologists querying the identification and validation of some of the more 'unusual' species and as a result some records were withdrawn or treated with caution. It was probably not until the first formal appointment by the Hertfordshire Natural History Society (HNHS) of Bryan Sage as County Recorder for Dragonflies in 1962 and his successors Tom Gladwin in 1975 and Christine Shepperson in 1999, that the scrutiny of Hertfordshire records was strengthened.

From 1946-61, following Bertram Lloyd's death in 1944, his wife Sylvia compiled regular reports on the county's dragonflies, which were published in the Transactions of the Hertfordshire Natural History Society. Just six dedicated recorders supplied the majority of the records. From 1962 onwards the County Recorder produced the annual reports.

Starting in 1996 Christine and Denis Shepperson toured the county gathering data on the dragonfly populations. Christine became joint recorder with Tom Gladwin in 1998 and sole recorder in 1999. In 1998 Christine used all the data they had collected, in addition to Hertfordshire data already on the national DARTER database, to produce *A Review of Dragonflies and Damselflies in Hertfordshire in 1992–1998*. This publication contained distribution maps for each of the species over the period 1992–98 supported by historical information where available.

The review was distributed to active recorders in the county and a number of British Dragonfly Society (BDS) members resident within the county. Not surprisingly, the review created a resurgence of interest in dragonfly recording. Shortly afterwards, Tom Gladwin and Christine Shepperson met with Alan Reynolds, who suggested that the increase in recording activity should make a countywide study viable. Alan offered to coordinate the activity to produce an Atlas of Hertfordshire's dragonflies.

The Hertfordshire Dragonfly Group (HDG) was formed on the 4th May 2000 to enlist support for the study and to facilitate coordination. Christine's initiative to publish *A Review of Dragonflies and Damselflies in Hertfordshire in 1992–1998* coupled with the formation of the HDG resulted in a significant increase in the number of observers submitting records as shown below.

*Number of recorders*

| 1990 | 8 | 1994 | 10 | 1998 | 18 |
|------|---|------|----|------|----|
| 1991 | 6 | 1995 | 12 | 1999 | 38 |
| 1992 | 7 | 1996 | 17 | 2000 | 46 |
| 1993 | 7 | 1997 | 17 | 2001 | 50 |

The HDG held indoor meetings, field meetings and training sessions and an Atlas planning meeting each autumn once the results from the previous summer had been analysed. The membership, which exceeded 100 people, was kept informed of the latest news and progress on the Atlas by a series of six-monthly newsletters, entitled *Brachytron*, edited by Alan Reynolds. Once the Atlas fieldwork was completed at the end of 2005 the HDG was dissolved.

The Atlas Project was very successful. Complete coverage of the 458 tetrads in the county was achieved in the planned six-year period and a grand total of 14,671 records were collected. This large number of records collected in a relatively short period in time allows authoritative statements to be made regarding the distribution of dragonflies in Hertfordshire. The results of the study are presented and discussed in the following chapters.

Chapter 2 presents a detailed history of dragonfly recording in the county from the first dragonfly list in 1835 up to the start of the Atlas in 2000.

Chapter 3 gives a brief history of the county's aquatic habitats and how they have changed in nature over the years.

Chapter 4 details the design of the Atlas Project, how it was planned, monitored and how coverage was measured.

Chapter 5 presents the major output of the study, the distribution of dragonflies in Hertfordshire. For each of the 19 regular breeding species there are notes on identification, behaviour and habitat preference, historical records and the Atlas distribution map.

Chapter 6 provides details of the evidence of dragonfly breeding in the county, in accordance with the criteria agreed by the Dragonfly Conservation Group (DCG) under the umbrella of the BDS.

Chapter 7 presents a flight table for Hertfordshire's dragonflies. With a large number of records at our disposal it has been possible to produce a flight table that is specific to the county's dragonflies.

Chapter 8 provides details of the rare migrants that have been recorded in the county irrespective of whether they were recorded during the Atlas period. For each species there are notes on identification, behaviour and habitat preference.

Although the primary objective of the Atlas Project was to produce distribution maps of all the regular breeding species, the data has also allowed analyses that identify the most recorded species, the most widely distributed species and the best sites. The results of these analyses are given in Chapter 9.

Chapter 10 provides detailed information on where to watch dragonflies in Hertfordshire, featuring the top ten sites (those with 16 species or more). For each site there is a map of how to get there and for the larger sites, a map of the site itself. The write-up also includes information on parking, access, a description of the site and some of the species that may be seen.

Appendix A provides a glossary of the terms used in the book.

Appendix B is a gazetteer, listing all the sites and their grid references from where the dragonfly records were collected.

Appendix C provides a list of all the sources of information.

It is intended that this book will become the reference for the status of dragonflies in Hertfordhire in the early part of the 21st century and it is hoped that it will stimulate and encourage newcomers to share an interest in these fantastic creatures and go out into the field to enjoy them in their natural habitats.


## Acknowledgements

By far the most important people in the Atlas Project are the 119 recorders who contributed their records over the six-year period of the study. Without their dedication, enthusiasm and support none of this could be possible. Our sincere thanks go to them all. A list of all the recorders in alphabetical order is given overleaf.

We also wish to thank Alison Harding (Assistant Librarian at The Natural History Museum at Tring) and the staff of The Entomological Library of the Natural History Museum, London, for locating and making available historic material, documents and publications in their care, and Bryan Sage for the loan of historic material in his possession. We are grateful to the North Hertfordshire Museums Services for permission to reproduce the map of the county's river systems from *Flora of Hertfordshire* (Dony 1967).

Our thanks also go to John Stevens (Southern Hawker, Lesser Emperor), Roger Pritchard (Variable Damselfly) and Andy Bradford (Keeled Skimmer) for their permission to use their photographs; to Steve Cham and Barry Reed for their valuable comments on the manuscript and to the Hertfordshire Biological Records Centre and Herts & Middlesex Wildlife Trust (HMWT) for permission to reproduce data from the reports on *The Hertfordshire Habitat Survey Project*.

Finally we are particularly grateful to Jack Fearnside who designed the book and prepared the artwork and Linda Smith at Hertfordshire Natural History Society for copy-editing and proof-reading the manuscript and managing the book through to publication.

The dragonfly recorders were:

| | | |
|---|---|---|
| N Agar | S Gorton | A Reynolds |
| P Allen | A Guilford | P Rhodes |
| D Anderson | J Halls | K Robinson |
| K Anderson | M Harris | G Russell |
| L Atkinson | S Harris | J Russell |
| T Austin | W Hatton | G Salisbury |
| S Avery | D Hawthorn | N Sampford |
| J Bater | M Hawthorn | D Sampson |
| J Baker | M Healy | B Sawford |
| H Baker | T Hill | S Saxton |
| G Barker | N Holmes-Smith | C Scott |
| B Bennett | G Hom | C Shepperson |
| C Best | A Horder | D Shepperson |
| J Best | P Hudson | J Shepperson |
| M Best | S Hughes | A Smith |
| A Bradford | T James | D Spring |
| S Brooks | M Jennings | A Stubbs |
| J Bunyan (1) | C Lambert | J Taylor |
| J Bunyan (2) | H Laming | E Tearle |
| M Campbell | S Lane | J Terry |
| T Chapman | D Leeming | B Trevis |
| D Coates | D Marriot | M Velasco |
| A Cockburn | K McLellan | G Vicary |
| B Cripps | A Middleton | A Walton |
| T Crown | J Moody | P Walton |
| J Dixon | J Moss | D Warner |
| D Dorken | S Murray | S Warrington |
| A Downie | C Nash (1) | D Wedd |
| J Doyle | C Nash (2) | K Weedon |
| C Everett | M Nash | M Weedon |
| A Fisher | M Noakes | J Wells |
| J Ford | J Noakes | M Wells |
| M Ford | P Oakenfull | G White |
| S Ford | D Pearson | J Widgery |
| V Fullforth | J Pearson | D Wingrove |
| J Gardiner | S Penn | A Wood |
| J Gladwin | S Pittman | R Woodward |
| T Gladwin | C Plant | J Worroll |
| D Gompertz | B Reed | I Wynne |
| E Goodyear | P Reeves | |

# 2. History of the dragonflies of Hertfordshire 1835-2006

The first published records of dragonflies identified in Hertfordshire are due to J F Stephens (1835). Born in Sussex, James Francis Stephens (1792-1852) was educated at the Blue Coat School, Hertford, and Christ's Hospital. It was in Hertford, to which he often returned in adult life, that he began his lifelong interest in British insects. In 1818 he assisted in arranging the British Museum's insect collection and later, following early retirement, worked there unpaid until his death. During his lifetime he described some 2,800 species native to Britain. He had a fine, catalogued collection of British insects, including a significant number taken in and around Hertford, most of which are in the British Museum.

In his *Illustrations of British Entomology; or a Synopsis of Indigenous Insects* (1828-46) he provides numerous records of insects from the county, including four of dragonflies (Vol VI, 1835) noting, first stating the synonyms used by Stephens, as follows:

**Emperor Dragonfly *Anax formosa* Vander Linden, 1823 (*A. imperator* Leach 1815).**
'Not uncommon in several parts of the country; also taken near Hertford.'

**Brown Hawker *Aeshna grandis* Linnaeus, 1758.**
'Abundant, during the summer and autumn... at Hertford.'

**Migrant Hawker *Aeshna affinis* Stephens, 1835 (*A. mixta* Latreille 1805).**
'A rather uncommon species or at least apparently so: found at Hertford, in July.'

**Hairy Dragonfly *Aeshna vernalis* Vander Linden, 1820 (*Brachytron pratense* Müller 1764).**
'Not very common... found at Hertford.'

Surprisingly, perhaps, no Hertfordshire records of damselflies (*Zygoptera*) are to be found in Stephens' accounts. Thereafter, little attention appears to have been given to the county's dragonflies throughout the Victorian period. Curiously the collecting and study of dragonflies was evidently not popular during the 19th century. Part of the reason may be the difficulty in preserving the colours of specimens. It was undoubtedly the publication of W Harcourt

Bath's *Illustrated Handbook of British Dragonflies* (1890) that stimulated more interest in these brightly coloured insects.

Although quoting Stephens (1835) as a source, W F Evans (1845) in *British Libellulinae: or Dragon Flies*, which illustrated the known British Odonata in a series of lithograph drawings, only lists the last three species named above as found in the county. Bath (1890), who also referred directly to Stephens' works, lists all four.

Lucas (1900) described 40 species as having been reported in Britain but doubted the validity of the Vagrant or Moustached Darter *Sympetrum vulgatum* (Linnaeus 1758) as a British species. In addition he described the national status of the Yellow-winged Darter *S. flaveolum* (Linnaeus 1758) and Red-veined Darter *S. fonscolombii* (Sélys 1840) as 'only occasional visitors'. Although he includes Stephens (1835) in his list or references, he evidently drew his Hertfordshire data from Evans (1845), whom he quotes, and so omits the Emperor Dragonfly from his list and also overlooks the reference to the Migrant Hawker. Thus he includes only the Brown Hawker and Hairy Dragonfly as Hertfordshire species from the four listed in earlier sources. In addition he lists Chipperfield Common as a locality for the inappropriately named Common Hawker *Aeshna juncea* (Linnaeus 1758) quoting J Arkle as his source. No details being provided, and no other reference being found in a search of national and local archives, it was not possible to authenticate this record. The lack of attention given to Hertfordshire dragonflies up to this time is illustrated by comparing Hertfordshire with the adjacent county of Essex for which Lucas (1900) lists no fewer than 28 species. Henry Doubleday (1871) had earlier listed 30 species as occurring 'in the neighbourhood of Epping' just five miles east of the boundary with Hertfordshire.

A E Gibbs in Page (1902), refers to the four species listed by Stephens (1835) as comprising the known Hertfordshire dragonfly fauna, and overlooks or omits the reference to the Common Hawker in Lucas (1900).

Speyer (1910 & 1911), who later worked in the Natural History section of the British Museum, published detailed records of 12 species, which he specifically identified in the county in the three-year period from 1908-10. These are the first county records, most of which are for 1908, for which details including dates, locations, and a statement of relative abundance are given. The 12 species he reported, all from Aldenham Reservoir and/or Shenley, and his general statements of relative abundance, were:

**Azure Damselfly *Coenagrion puella* (Linnaeus 1758)***
'At Shenley, plentiful in 1908, and common there in 1909 and 1910.'

**Common Blue Damselfly *Enallagma cyathigerum* (Charpentier 1840)***
'Very common in Hertfordshire in 1908, and plentiful at Shenley in 1909.'

**Blue-tailed Damselfly *Ischnura elegans* (Vander Linden 1820)***
'Plentiful at Shenley in 1908 where the female variety *rufescens* was "taken abundantly" together with a single specimen of variety *infuscans*, abundant there in 1909, and common in 1910.'

**Red-eyed Damselfly *Erythromma najas* (Hansemann 1823)***
'Abundant at Aldenham Reservoir and Shenley in 1908, only sparingly at the latter location in 1909 but common there in 1910.'

**Southern Hawker *Aeshna cyanea* (Müller 1764)***
'Common in Hertfordshire during August and September.'

**Brown Hawker *A. grandis* (Linnaeus 1758)**
'Abundant at Shenley in 1908.'

**Emperor Dragonfly *Anax imperator* (Leach 1815)**
'A male and two females captured in a gravel-pit near Shenley on 24th June 1908, and one seen there on 29th July 1909, and very common at Shenley in 1910.'

**Four-spotted Chaser *Libellula quadrimaculata* (Linnaeus 1758)***
'A male captured at Shenley on 19th July 1909.'

**Broad-bodied Chaser *L. depressa* (Linnaeus 1758)***
'Abundant at Shenley in 1908, and common there in 1910.'

**Black-tailed Skimmer *Orthetrum cancellatum* (Linnaeus, 1758)***
'A female and a male obtained at Aldenham Reservoir on 27th and 29th July 1908, respectively.'

**Common Darter *Sympetrum striolatum* (Charpentier 1840)***
'Common around Shenley in 1908, and observed there up to 21st October 1909.'

**Red-veined Darter *S. fonscolombii* (Sélys 1840)***
'Two captured near Shenley on 24th June, and a female netted at Aldenham Reservoir on 27th July 1908.'

The ten species marked with an asterisk (*) are the first published records of these for the county. Interestingly Speyer's records do not include any reference to the Migrant Hawker but he does, perhaps unusually, refer to the Southern Hawker as being common in September.

A E Gibbs contributed the section on dragonflies in Hopkinson (1911), which is based on a list of 18 species which had been 'furnished' to him by Speyer and which were said to have been 'taken' at Shenley. The list, included in full, is qualified by Gibbs with the statement that 'probably some of these were found just outside the area covered by these notes'. A wise precaution indeed, for a search of the local archives by Gladwin, and subsequent to his earlier review (Gladwin 1997(b)), found evidence that Speyer's list, dated 1907, and probably written from memory, included species for which he had made detailed notes of observations at Tunbridge Wells, Kent, but not evidently for Hertfordshire. These included the Golden-ringed Dragonfly *Cordulegaster boltonii* (Donovan 1807 (*annulatus* Latreille 1805)), Keeled Skimmer *Orthetrum coerulescens* (Fabricius 1798), Ruddy Darter *Sympetrum sanguineum* (Müller 1764), and Black Darter *S. danae* (Sulzer 1776 (*scoticum* Donovan 1811)).

The last two might be expected to have been present in the county in the early part of the 20th century but Hopkinson's and Speyer's lists provide no certain evidence of this. In later correspondence copied by Bryan Sage, the Recorder for Dragonflies from 1962-75, Speyer advised that there were some unfortunate errors in the list he supplied Gibbs. Further, in the case of three other species named in the lists, ie the Emerald Damselfly *Lestes sponsa* (Hansemann 1823), Large Red Damselfly *Pyrrhosoma nymphula* (Sulzer 1776), and Yellow-winged Darter, the records would be the first to be published for the county. No details are given, except that the Large Red Damselfly was reported as 'observed in June 1905, when it was rather plentiful' but without any mention of the location(s).

The lists also include the sole but erroneous British record of the Green Emerald Damselfly *Lestes viridis* (Vander Linden 1825). The record is based on a correctly identified male, formerly in the British Museum, labelled as captured by E R Speyer at Shenley (Herts) on 11th August 1899. Speyer had been working in Belgium that year and later considered it possible that the specimen had been incorrectly labelled (Sage 1961; Gladwin 1997(b), 1997(c)). Thus the Green Emerald Dragonfly was removed from the British and Hertfordshire lists.

Lucas (1904) wrote as follows; 'Some months back Mr E R Speyer sent me for examination a male *Lestes*, which he took on August 11th 1899, flying swiftly over an alder-bush on the side of a large lake at Shenley, Herts. It arrived in fragments, but the appendages left no doubt as to its being *Lestes viridis*; but I should rather hesitate to add it to the British list till more specimens are captured. Perhaps this note will cause others to search for it next season. It is already reputed to be British but the evidence is not sufficient.' Lucas, the author of the then definitive work *British Dragonflies* (1900), returned the specimen to Speyer advising him of his decision. It is therefore surprising that this record continued to be included, without qualification, in lists produced by Speyer and others for many years thereafter.

A drawing of the appendages of the specimen is included in Lucas (1904).

The inclusion of the Banded Demoiselle *Calopteryx splendens* (Harris 1782) in Hopkinson (1911) as a Hertfordshire species is based on it having been 'taken by Miss Alice Dickinson in the Lea valley, between Harpenden and Wheathampstead'. The archives show that at least one specimen was passed to Gibbs who deposited it 'in the Hertfordshire County Museum' (St Albans) where he curated the insect collections. Gibbs was by then clearly aware of all the earlier sources referred to above, as he correctly states that the addition of the Banded Demoiselle brought the number of species recorded as having been observed in the county to 24. Thus he included the record of the Common Hawker he either omitted or overlooked nine years earlier (Gibbs 1902), and all records due to Speyer.

It may be asked why, when he was so meticulous in recording the collections in his care, Gibbs was not more questioning about the information supplied by Speyer? The answer lies in the fact that in that era views tended to be expressed in a rather more coded and subtle form than is the case nearly 100 years later. Thus his qualification of Speyer's list, 'probably some of these were found just outside the area covered by these notes', was both cautionary and, as is now known, correct. He also acknowledged the list supplied to Hopkinson to be deficient in that it lacked detail and authentication, and should therefore be treated accordingly.

Gibbs, also in Hopkinson (1911), records the Golden-ringed Dragonfly as occurring in his garden at Kitchener's Meads. Dragonflies, it should be noted, were one order of insects in which he was least interested. More generally identification aids were not widely available at that time, and observers may have easily confused Common Hawkers, Migrant Hawkers, Southern Hawkers and Golden-ringed Dragonflies. Even relatively recently, Stephen Brooks (1989), the author of *Field Guide to the Dragonflies and Damselflies of Great Britain and Ireland* (1997), wrote of the Common Hawker in his paper *The Dragonflies (*Odonata*) of London* (1989), 'that it is apparent the species is frequently confused with *A. mixta* and *A. cyanea*'. Thus in 1996 the present writer (Tom Gladwin) and Steve Brooks together reviewed all past records of the Common Hawker in Hertfordshire and found some, including two due to Tom Gladwin, to be certainly the subject of incorrect identification (Gladwin 1997(b)).

By 1911, and apart from a specimen in the British Museum labelled as taken at Tring on 1st October 1901, there had been no records of the Migrant Hawker since that of Stephens (1835) 76 years earlier. Was it rare, as Henry Doubleday described it in Essex (Lucas 1900), or overlooked? It was not then established as a resident species in southeast England but did occur as a regular migrant from the continent.

Between 1920 and 1940 the records of three observers collectively provide the first overview of the dragonfly fauna of Hertfordshire during that period.

D G Sevastopoulo (in Wainwright 1926), whose notes have fortunately survived, provided information about nine species observed on and around Hertford Heath and in the Lower Lea and Stort Valleys between Stanstead Abbotts and Broxbourne. Ray Palmer (1930 & 1940) published lists including 20 species observed in north, central and southwest Hertfordshire. Bertram Lloyd's three papers (1937, 1938 & 1939) provided information on the status of 14 species he identified in the southwest of the county. Among the particularly important sites he visited were Elstree (Aldenham) Reservoir, the River Colne, and the Lily Pool at Wall Hall, near Aldenham. The records of these three observers are collectively summarised in the Table 1 below. Using the relative terms adopted by the three observers, the table gives a useful overview of the county's dragonfly fauna at that earlier time. It is, of course, an overview that has to be interpreted in relation to the amount of appropriate habitat available to each species when the observations were made.

From the 'snapshot' that the table provides, it is evident that Hertfordshire's waterways had by then mostly recovered from the heavy burdens of untreated sewage that polluted them. This had continued well into the second half of the 19th century and, in some cases, beyond. Further it relates to a period before the intensive use of modern agro-chemicals that have polluted waterways since the Second World War. These statements are also true of the Grand Union Canal for which there are records of Banded Demoiselles, Brown Hawkers, and Common Darters in 1936.

As shown in Table 1, the Red-eyed Damselfly, Downy Emerald *Cordulia aenea* (Linnaeus 1758), Black-tailed Skimmer, and Ruddy Darter were each found at just one or two sites, and the Four-spotted Chaser rarely seen. The last two Downy Emeralds observed in the county, described by Longfield (1949(b)) as to be 'seen occasionally at Radlett, Aldenham, Shenley and Bricket Wood', were both caught and released during a field meeting of the HNHS at Aldenham on 28th July 1956. The populations of the other four species have all since increased. The observation of the Hairy Dragonfly in the Lea Valley, where Stephens (1835) had found it, is also of particular interest.

The identification and increasing populations of Migrant Hawkers from 1936 onwards, coincides with this species beginning its establishment as a resident in southeast England. Prior to that, the status of the Scarce Aeshna, as Cynthia Longfield (1949(b)) called it, was solely as a regular migrant from the continent.

The omission of species listed by Speyer (per Gibbs in Hopkinson 1911) from the papers by Palmer (1930 & 1940), and Bertram Lloyd (1937 & 1938), was deliberate. Gladwin (1997(b)) surmised that Ray Palmer, and Bertram and Sylvia Lloyd, 'were seemingly unaware of Gibbs' list'. Subsequent investigation has found that all three were in possession of Hopkinson (1911) and therefore knew that most of the species listed were solely due to Speyer. They were also aware of the latter's two papers in *The Entomologist* (Speyer 1910 & 1911). Bertram Lloyd's copy of Lucas (1900), now in the possession of Bryan Sage,

| Species | North Herts[1] | Central Herts[2] | East Herts[3] | South West Herts[4] |
|---|---|---|---|---|
| Banded Demoiselle | Rare/occasional | Abundant | Present | Fairly common |
| Large Red Damselfly | Very local | Locally scarce | | Abundant |
| Red-eyed Damselfly | | | | One site at Aldenham |
| Azure Damselfly | Common/abundant | Abundant | Common | Widespread |
| Variable Damselfly | | Hatfield 1929 | Woodhall Park 1924 | |
| Common Blue Damselfly | Very common | Very common | Along the Lea | Abundant |
| Blue-tailed Damselfly | Fairly common | Fairly common | Common | Widespread |
| Migrant Hawker | | | | Elstree Reservoir 1936-7 |
| Southern Hawker | Common | Common | Common | Common |
| Brown Hawker | | Present | Common | Common |
| Emperor Dragonfly | Not common | Scarce | Not common | Not common |
| Hairy Dragonfly | | | Not common | |
| Downy Emerald | | Knebworth 1922 | | Aldenham and Bricket Wood 1937 |
| Four-spotted Chaser | Very rare | Digswell 1921 | | Radlett (date?) |
| Broad-bodied Chaser | Common/abundant | Common/abundant | Common | Common |
| Black-tailed Skimmer | | | | Elstree Reservoir 1935-7 |
| Common Darter | Abundant | Abundant | Common | Abundant |
| Yellow-winged Darter | | | | Bricket Wood 1926 |
| Ruddy Darter | | | | Bricket Wood 1938 |
| Black Darter | | Digswell 1929 | | |

*Table 1: Recorded status of dragonfly species observed in Hertfordshire between 1920 and 1939 by D G Sevastapoulo (in Wainwright 1926), R Palmer (1939 & 1940), and B Lloyd (1937, 1938 and 1939).*

**Notes for Table 1**

1 North Herts records from Oughtonhead Common, Hitchin, Ickleford and Stevenage.

2 Central Herts records from Digswell, Knebworth, Tewin, Welwyn, Welwyn Garden City and Wheathampstead.

3 East Herts records from the area around Hertford Heath and Lower Lea and Stort Valleys between Stanstead Abbotts and Broxbourne.

4 South West Herts records from Aldenham, Bushey, Bricket Wood, Elstree, Radlett and Shenley.

provides some evidence as it is annotated with a few of Speyer's records. Some are qualified with exclamation marks (!) suggesting they should be treated with caution. Palmer (1940) mentions Speyer's record of a Red-veined Darter at Elstree in 1908, but does not include the source (Speyer 1910) or Hopkinson (1911) in his accompanying list of references. Further, Palmer, in his unpublished notes on the specimens he examined in the Hertfordshire County Museum in St Albans, queries the capture of a Golden-ringed Dragonfly from Gibbs' garden with the annotation '*Aeshna cyanea*'. It is evident, therefore, that both Ray Palmer and Bertram Lloyd viewed many of the earlier records as uncertain.

Palmer (1930) in his first paper on *Dragonflies Observed in Hertfordshire*, which was also reproduced in Hine (1934), refers to having 'reared large numbers of Southern Hawkers in his garden pond'. Thus the breeding of this species in gardens, urban and rural, is not new. Although the Southern Hawker was the commonest large hawker in the 1930s, it has continued to increase in numbers due at least as much to the proliferation of garden ponds as to the expansion of flooded mineral workings.

In his second paper on *Hertfordshire's Dragonflies* Palmer (1940) includes references to five species not included in Table 1, namely; the White-legged Damselfly *Platycnemis pennipes* (Pallas 1771), Common Hawker, Club-tailed Dragonfly *Gomphus vulgatissimus* (Linnaeus 1758), Red-veined Darter and Vagrant Darter *Sympetrum vulgatum* (Linnaeus 1758).

The inclusion of the White-legged Damselfly was based on a reference to one at Northaw on 11th August 1934 (Attlee 1935). In a letter dated 25th July 1941, a copy of which is filed with Tom Gladwin, Attlee advised that this was the subject of a typographical error, and the site of his record should read Newhaw in Surrey (Lloyd B 1942). It was eight years later, in 1942 that the White-legged Damselfly was first found in Hertfordshire, when it was discovered at Tring (Lloyd B 1944) and on the Lea Canal near Broxbourne (Hayward & Hayward 1945).

The inclusion in Palmer (1940) of the Common Hawker and Red-veined Darter are each based on single records discussed earlier, ie those of Arkle (undated in Lucas 1900) and Speyer at Elstree in 1908 respectively.

The references to the Club-tailed Dragonfly and Vagrant Darter in Palmer (1940) were drawn from *The Dragonflies of the British Isles* (Longfield 1937) in which 'Hertford' is listed as one of the counties in which they had been observed. Following correspondence with Palmer the reference to the Club-tailed Dragonfly does not appear in the second edition of the book (Longfield 1949(a)). In the same correspondence Longfield advised Palmer that she had a record of the Vagrant Darter taken at Tring in August 1901, but unfortunately no note of the authority. Palmer published the record with the rider that 'there has been much confusion between this and the Common Darter'. Significantly Cynthia Longfield, aware of Lucas (1904), made no reference to Speyer's specimen of the Green Emerald Dragonfly mistakenly labelled as having been captured at Shenley in 1899.

Bertram Lloyd's paper *West Hertfordshire Dragonflies* (1944) added significantly to the knowledge of dragonflies in and around Tring Reservoirs and along the Aylesbury Arm of the Grand Union Canal. The species he observed breeding there included Migrant Hawker (common), Four-spotted Chaser (for the first time in Herts), White-legged Damselfly (abundant) and a small colony of Red-eyed Damselflies along the Aylesbury Arm in 1942. The latter was only the second breeding site for this species to be found in the county. A year later in 1943 a colony was found on the Lea Canal near Cheshunt (Hayward & Hayward 1945).

From 1946 to 1961, following Bertram Lloyd's death in 1944, his wife Sylvia studied and provided reports on dragonflies seen in the county. The appearance of a Ruddy Darter, or Scarce Crimson Dragonfly as she called it, at Elstree in 1946 (Lloyd S 1948) prompted her to correspond with Cynthia Longfield who considered it to be a probable immigrant, and advised of several at a pond in Cowheath Wood, Broxbourne, in the same year. Also in 1946, a single Common Hawker was recorded at Chipperfield on 10th September.

In her paper, *The Dragonflies* (Odonata) *of the London Area*, Cynthia Longfield (1949(b)) includes the Emerald Damselfly, Scarce Emerald Damselfly *Lestes dryas* (Kirby 1890) and Keeled Skimmer *Orthetrum coerulescens* (Fabricius 1798) in her list of Hertfordshire species. Of the Emerald Dragonfly she states 'it has been known from the northwestern side of our boundary since the beginning of the century but is only really abundant at one water'. Neither Steve Brooks nor Tom Gladwin, former recorders of dragonflies for the London Area and Hertfordshire respectively, were able to trace the source of this statement on the Emerald Damselfly although the species was in Speyer's list included by Gibbs in Hopkinson (1911). Unbeknown to Longfield, G E Winbolt (1949) had discovered a small breeding colony at ponds on Hertford Heath on 1st June 1947, and claimed this to be the first record of the species in the county. Four years later, in 1951, he found larvae of the species at the same ponds.

Regarding the Scarce Emerald Dragonfly, a colonising species mostly found in densely vegetated ditches and pools, Cynthia Longfield's statement that it had become established at a new locality in the county, in 1946, almost certainly refers to the pond by Elstree Reservoir where C O Hammond caught one in that year.

The Keeled Skimmer is recorded as being observed in Hertfordshire on four occasions, ie at Shenley, where it was 'not captured', prior to 1911 (Hopkinson 1911); Hatfield Great Wood in 1945 (Hodgson 1959), and a female captured at Wilstone Reservoir, Tring, on 30th August 1952 (Lloyd S 1954). Sylvia Lloyd (1954) placed all three records in square brackets [ ]. She stated that the last should be accepted with caution and the localities of the first two were unsuited to the species' normal habits. Cynthia Longfield, in correspondence with S B Hodgson, advised that her statement (1949(b)) that 'in Herts it can still be found in two districts' was entirely based on the first of these records. Hodgson's paper on *West Hertfordshire Dragonflies* (1959) was very well researched and typically cautious in its treatment. Thus he also placed all three records in square brackets [ ]. Finally Steve Brooks, in *The Dragonflies (Odonata) of London: the Current Status* (1989), whilst recognising the possibility that the Keeled Skimmer may once have been found on 'one of the heaths near St Albans or Hertford' consistently treats all early records of this species as uncertain. There is no doubt, however, about the fourth record. One was photographed by Andy Bradford at a pond in Grove Millenium Wood, near Bishops Stortford, on 10th July 2003.

G E Winbold (1949 & 1950) observed the Large Red Damselfly to be common around Haileybury, Red-eyed Damselflies common on the Lea at Broxbourne, the Migrant Hawker to have become common in recent years, and the Emperor Dragonfly present at several sites. He reported the Ruddy Darter as having been seen in the Haileybury area for the first time in 1947 and to be quite well distributed at ponds on Hertford Heath and along the Roman Road. The Hairy Dragonfly having 'not been seen around the college (Haileybury) in recent years' he queried the earlier record, ie that of Sevastapoulo (in Wainwright 1926) as a possible error. Fortunately the evidence validating that record is provided in Wainwright's annotated copy of *The Fauna and Flora of Haileybury*. The Hairy Dragonfly had disappeared from the Hertfordshire scene, although it was found along the Aylesbury Canal in 1950, and continued to be observed there and at Tring for some years thereafter. On 24th May 1992, Tom and Janet Gladwin observed one at Cook's Wood, Burnham Green. Since then it has become re-established as a regular breeding species in the county.

E R Speyer (1949) published details of a mature male Scarce Blue-tailed Damselfly *Ischnura pumilio* (Charpentier, 1825) he captured on 4th August 1948, 'by the side of a waterfall to the north of Hertford'. Identification was confirmed by D E Kimmins at the British Museum (Nat Hist) where Speyer was working at the time and where the specimen was deposited. It is now known that Cynthia Longfield also inspected the specimen and questioned Speyer as to the precise location where it was collected. Fortunately her notes, which she copied to S B Hodgson, survived showing that she satisfied herself as to the suitability of the habitat; a series of spring-fed boggy areas below some old gravel workings. As a result she effectively authenticated it by including details of the record in her paper on *The Dragonflies (Odonata) of the London Area* (Longfield 1949(b)) although the record was not within that area.

Regular reports on the county's dragonflies for the 15 years from 1947 to 1961 were compiled by Sylvia Lloyd and published in *Trans Herts NHS*. The great majority of records reported were supplied by just six dedicated observers, namely H H S Hayward (from 1947-60), J N Hobbs (1950-2), S B Hodgson (1955-61), L Lloyd-Evans (1955-61), B L Sage (1951-61), and herself. The records she received enabled her to detect significant changes in some populations. Ruddy Darters and Migrant Hawkers were noted as increasing. The latter, sometimes reported as forming 'clouds', were seen ovipositing for the first time in 1955.

Black-tailed Skimmers were found at several new locations, mostly newly flooded and ecologically immature waters such as Hilfield Park Reservoir, the lagoons at Rye Meads Sewage Purification Works and Stanstead Abbotts Gravel Pits. Emerald Damselflies, White-legged Damselflies, Large Red Damselflies, Red-eyed Damselflies and Four-spotted Chasers, each maintained breeding populations at a small number of sites.

Sylvia Lloyd's reports contained records of several scarce and rare species. In 1946 C O Hammond had collected one of a small number of Scarce Emerald Damselflies he had observed at a pond adjacent to Elstree Reservoir. Bryan Sage reported finding seven at the same site on 26th July 1952 and 15 on 4th July 1953. In 1956 L Lloyd-Evans found a small but flourishing colony on Hertford Heath. Two years later, in 1958, he discovered the colony on Patmore Heath where it outnumbered the Emerald Damselfly. Interestingly, both Ruddy Darters and Emerald Damselflies were present at all three sites. All the sites were severally visited in 1961 and 1962. The pond at Elstree had apparently been infilled. No Scarce Emerald Damselflies were found, and the species was considered to be extinct in the county.

In 1956 Lloyd-Evans found Black Darters breeding at the acid ponds on Patmore Heath where the population survived until at least 1975. The site continued to be monitored for this species and it was not found again until Brian Sawford rediscovered it there in September 1987. Black Darters were also observed at Smallford for three years from 1970-72. The only other authenticated records are of one seen by Bryan Sage at Ardeley on 11th September 1975, and one by Alan Reynolds at Hertford Heath on 28th July 2002.

Publishing the record of a Beautiful Demoiselle *Calopteryx virgo* observed on the Wendover Arm of the Grand Union Canal, near Little Tring Reservoir, by Bryan Sage on 30th August 1959, Sylvia Lloyd said she had 'seen a few in Cassiobury Park before the war'. However, there is no reference to this species in any of her husband's, Bertram Lloyd, papers.

The only record of the Small Red Damselfly *Ceriagrion tenellum* (de Villiers, 1789) is of 'three females and one male seen by the River Beane on 19th July (1959), the male and one female *in copulo*', which Sylvia Lloyd (1961 & 1962) published without comment. Of this Gladwin (1997(b)) wrote, 'none were captured and thus examined, and no detailed descriptions were provided. It is a species which breeds on wet heathland and peaty pools in bogs and mires. A very weak flyer, it is not known to move far from the breeding sites. Consultation with other recorders, and an extensive search of the main literature, has found no evidence of this species breeding in atypical habitats such as those on the floodplain of the River Beane. Sufficient uncertainty must therefore attach to this record that the Small Red Damselfly cannot confidently be treated as a Hertfordshire species'.

From 1962-75 Bryan Sage produced regular reports on the dragonflies observed in the county. For the first 11 years he received reports from never more than eight observers. The years 1973-75 saw a sudden surge of interest with 33 observers submitting reports for all or some of those years.

The late 60s and early 70s saw a decline in many dragonfly populations resulting from the construction of flood prevention schemes, involving the canalisation of some waterways, agricultural intensification and pollution with agro-chemicals and, in some cases, heavy metals. The chemistry of some waterways was changed by the increased discharge of treated sewage effluent as towns and villages expanded to accommodate huge population increases. Its effect on dragonfly populations does not seem to have been assessed.

Flows from many springs ceased as a result of increased water abstraction from aquifers and the consequential reduction of flows in streams and rivers caused the silting, shallowing and narrowing of watercourses. The upper sections of most of the county's chalk streams (eg Gade, Ver, Mimram, Beane and Rib) dried up completely. Flows became and remain so low that, ecologically as indicated by changes in their invertebrate fauna, some streams and rivers more often resemble linear ponds.

During this period the Aylesbury Arm of the Grand Union Canal was of great importance in continuing to support populations of Red-eyed Damselflies, Emerald Damselflies, White-legged Damselflies, Hairy Dragonflies (occasional) and Ruddy Darters which were to be found, if at all, at very few other sites. Large Red Damselflies were largely restricted to ponds on Hertford Heath and in woodlands at Bramfield, Broxbourne and Wormley. Rarely observed elsewhere, Four-spotted Chasers were only found breeding at ponds in Broad Riding and Broxbourne Wood.

In 1969 Bruce Ing discovered a small population of the Variable Damselfly *Coenagrion pulchellum* (Vander Linden 1825) at a pond in Watery Grove, Stevenage. One was caught and the identification confirmed. The species could not be found following extensive management of the pond in the spring of 1971. The only other authenticated record is of a male photographed and identified by Roger Pritchard near a spring-fed moat at Westbury, Ashwell, on 28th June 1996.

No fewer than 17 records of Common Hawkers were published in the reports covering the 15-year period from 1951-65. The biological recording area of the London Natural History Society (LNHS) is defined as the area within a 20-mile radius of St Paul's Cathedral, which approximately includes the southern one-third of Hertfordshire. Arrangements have long existed whereby the HNHS and LNHS exchange records for the area of common interest. Concerned at the number of published historic records lacking important detail, and the continuing misidentification of Common Hawkers, the respective recorders, Tom Gladwin and Steve Brooks, met in 1985 to decide how best to evaluate such information. They agreed that all records lacking important detail, such as observer, date and precise location, and those of rare species that did not include validatory evidence, would be classed as 'uncertain' for the purposes of the scientific record.

In respect of the records of Common Hawkers only those from Cuffley Greatwood on 27th August 1959, Rye Meads (caught) on 27th August 1964, several captures of one (photographed) in mist nets at the acid ponds in a heathy area of Bramfield Forest in 1969 and another at the same site on 7th September 1971, were found to satisfy the criteria agreed by the two recorders. Bramfield, from where there was no evidence of breeding, is outside the area covered by the LNHS. The record of one in 1981, previously shown as the last to be recorded in Hertfordshire, was subsequently withdrawn following publication of Gladwin (1997(b)). At best this has always been a very rare species in the county. All records of the Common Hawker submitted since 1971 have been the subject of some uncertainty.

Tom Gladwin succeeded Bryan Sage as recorder for dragonflies in 1976. Aware of the decline in populations he and his wife Janet decided to personally survey the less common and scarce species. The results of their fieldwork were detailed in his report on dragonflies for the years 1976-83 (Gladwin 1983) which was accidentally omitted from *Trans Herts NHS*, and distributed privately, and in subsequent periodic reports. In 1986 he commenced an annual census of populations at the then Amwell Quarry (now Amwell Nature Reserve). Based on a network of fixed transects and including measurements of habitat development and change, the survey in 2007 is in its 22nd year.

In addition to those along the Aylesbury Arm of the Grand Union Canal, Tom and Janet Gladwin found only small numbers of White-legged Damselflies at one other site, at Cheshunt in 1981. Populations, which unpublished records show had variously existed upstream along the Lea as far as Hertford, and at Waterford and Panshanger on the Beane and Mimram respectively, had disappeared. There is no doubt that this species had been adversely affected by flood alleviation and canalisation works along the Lea. In 1985 Graham White (1986) reported the population at Cheshunt to be 'strong' and it maybe that it had only recently become established there. By 1987 it had reappeared on the Lea at Amwell Quarry only to disappear again following river works in 1990.

Tom and Janet Gladwin's survey found Ruddy Darters at only five sites. Red-eyed Damselflies had appeared along the Lea and Stort Valleys, and at a few sites in the middle part of the Colne Valley, and Large Red Damselflies had colonised ponds and expanded their range in the south of the county. It was evident that populations of most species were increasing. In 1994 Steve Brooks confirmed that he had successfully reared Ruddy Darters at his

St Albans home from larvae collected in 1993 from a pond at Bricket Wood. The success of this experiment might encourage similar projects with the object of securing populations of rare vulnerable weak-flying non-migratory species, eg Small Red Damselfly, which by virtue of their relative isolation might, on examination, be found to exhibit distinct geographic variations.

The year 1995 was particularly memorable for the large numbers of migrant darters reaching Britain. In Hertfordshire, Yellow-winged Darters were observed at 17 different sites in August, and ovipositing observed at Amwell Quarry (now Amwell Nature Reserve), Hertford Heath, Panshanger, and Wilstone Reservoir, Tring. The largest numbers counted were 25 at Hertford Heath on 20th, 13 at Amwell Quarry on 12th, and 10 at Wilstone Reservoir from 5th to 21st, and Hilfield Park Reservoir and Panshanger on 12th August. Two Vagrant Darters, the first authenticated records for the county, were also observed during this period. Tom and Janet Gladwin caught and photographed a male at Panshanger on 12th August and Stephen Smith provided a detailed description of one he observed at Tyttenhanger the following day. Very much larger numbers than usual of Ruddy Darters suggested this species to have also been involved in the immigration.

Details of some of the 1995 immigrants were included in lists of Hertfordshire records kindly supplied for some years by Ruth Day who had succeeded Steve Brooks as the LNHS Recorder for Dragonflies for the London Area.

The huge amount of new information generously provided by Steve Murray throughout the 1990s was of great significance in drawing attention to, and enabling rapidly changing populations and distributions to be monitored and evaluated. The Red-veined Darter observed by him at Hilfield Park Reservoir on 22nd May 1992 was the first to be seen in the county for many years. Other regular contributors of large numbers of records in the 1990s included Trevor James, then in charge of the Hertfordshire Biological Records Centre, Mike Harris who carried out a comprehensive survey of dragonflies at Rye Meads in 1996, Tom Gladwin who surveyed populations at Panshanger from 1992-97, Graham White and Christine and Denis Shepperson.

For ten years from 1996 through the period of the Atlas survey (2000-05) Christine and Denis Shepperson dedicated themselves to gathering data on dragonfly populations across the whole county. Christine became joint recorder with Tom Gladwin in 1998 and sole recorder from 1999. In 1998 and 1999 she produced and privately published two detailed and very important reports, *A Review of Dragonflies and Damselflies in Hertfordshire 1992-1998* (Shepperson C 1998) and *A Review of Dragonflies in Hertfordshire in 1999* (Shepperson C 1999). These reports were distributed to everybody contributing records and all Hertfordshire-based members of the British Dragonfly Society. Using data from the Darter database and Dmap, Steve Cham supplied tetrad based distribution maps for all breeding species. The reports provide an invaluable snapshot of the status of the county's dragonflies at the end of the 20th century.

In 1999 Tom Gladwin and Christine Shepperson formulated proposals for a book on Hertfordshire's dragonflies. Shortly afterwards they met with Alan Reynolds who suggested and offered to organise a comprehensive survey of the whole county which would logically continue and expand on Christine's work. The results of the survey would be an atlas of Hertfordshire's dragonflies. It was agreed that such an atlas would be of great importance in identifying sites deserving of statutory and local designations for reasons of their dragonfly interest, deciding priorities for conservation measures, and informing management plans.

*Azure Damselfly*

A strategy was agreed and, in order to create interest and provide a vehicle for the survey, it was decided to form The Hertfordshire Dragonfly Group. On the 4th May 2000 Tom Gladwin chaired a well-attended meeting held in Digswell Village Church Hall at which the HDG was formed. The agreed objectives of the HDG were:

(a) To monitor key species such as the Hairy Dragonfly and White-legged Damselfly.

(b) To monitor key sites, possibly by the use of transects.

(c) To carry out a survey in preparation for a Hertfordshire Dragonfly Atlas over the period 2000-05.

During the survey the interest of the many members and other observers who contributed to the Atlas was sustained by holding indoor meetings and through ten issues of a newsletter, *Brachytron*, which also included articles on topical subjects. *Brachytron* took its name from the Hairy Dragonfly, then the county's latest breeding species, for which exuviae had been found below the former railway bridge at Amwell Quarry by Tom and Janet Gladwin in May and June 1999. In 2002, during the survey, which was entirely organised by Alan Reynolds and Christine Shepperson, one new species, the Small Red-eyed Damselfly *Erythromma viridulum* (Charpentier 1840), was added to the Hertfordshire fauna.

In summary, sufficient authentication exists to be certain that the following 30 species have occurred in Hertfordshire, of which those 19 marked with an asterisk (*) regularly breed.

Beautiful Demoiselle

Banded Demoiselle*

Emerald Damselfly*

Scarce Emerald Damselfly

White-legged Damselfly*

Large Red Damselfly*

Red-eyed Damselfly*

Small Red-eyed Damselfly*

Azure Damselfly*

Variable Damselfly

Common Blue Damselfly*

Scarce Blue-tailed Damselfly

Blue-tailed Damselfly*

Hairy Dragonfly*

Common Hawker

Migrant Hawker*

Southern Hawker*

Brown Hawker*

Emperor Dragonfly*

Downy Emerald

Four-spotted Chaser*

Broad-bodied Chaser*

Black-tailed Skimmer*

Keeled Skimmer

Common Darter*

Ruddy Darter*

Black Darter

Yellow-winged Darter

Red-veined Darter

Vagrant Darter

# 3. Hertfordshire's aquatic habitats

In the late Middle Ages Hertfordshire's aquatic habitats mostly comprised ponds. Many of these were in the extensive tracts of semi-natural deciduous wood-pastures created in that part of the Forest of Middlesex that once covered much of the southern part of the county, villages and other settlements. Also important were the two major lowland river systems, ie the Lea with Stort, and the Colne, and their associated valley bottom mires and marshes. These major rivers were then, as now, fed by a series of fast south flowing, relatively shallow, chalk streams originating from the foot of the down-slopes of the Chilterns.

The county's flood plains were subject to regular seasonal inundation. Water tables were continuously at maximum height, and water extraction and man-made drainage insignificant. Reflecting the surface geology, most ponds, which were used for watering livestock, were located on the heavy clays where they were easily constructed by digging into or 'puddling' the impervious material. By 1600 pastures and cornfields had become an extensive part of the Hertfordshire scene. The land being wet, the conversion to pasture and arable often necessitated extensive drainage, which resulted in the creation of new marshlands and watercourses.

On the London Clays most of the resulting wetlands would have been acid in character. Other lentic, ie static or slow moving, aquatic habitats that might have held locally important dragonfly populations at that time were the moats and fish-ponds created around early settlements, and particularly on large estates and monastic properties. The extent to which acid heathland and associated ponds became established on areas from which the natural woodland had been cleared is uncertain, depending on the interpretation of early records of 'woodland' or 'waste'. As there were no large bodies of open water at this time, it is interesting to speculate that in mediaeval and Tudor times the dragonfly fauna of Hertfordshire may have been less diverse than at the end of the 20th century.

Apart from sections of the Lee Navigation, the first new major waterway to be constructed in Hertfordshire was the New River. The project, designed by Edmund Colthurst and largely constructed by Hugh Myddelton, was intended 'for bringing to the city of London a new Cutt or River of fresh Water' (Ward 2003). The first three miles from Chadwell Spring were dug in 1603. Work was halted from 1604-09, and the river finally completed in 1613. In a letter to Sir Robert Cecil in 1602 Colthurst stated, 'The water I mean to bring is spring and no part of the River Lee'. Thus it is evident that the river was at first intended to deliver water solely from the springs at Amwell and Chadwell. However by 1613 a connection had been completed to the River Lea, from which up to 22.5 million gallons were being drawn daily.

In Saxon times 'large boats' were able to navigate up the River Lea as far as Hertford. By 1600 the river had narrowed and become shallower and, despite the construction of new locks and weirs in 1571, was only navigable by shallow barges, which mostly transported grain from Ware to London. The situation was worsened by the diversion of water into the New River. In 1739 new locks were built at Broxbourne, Stanstead Abbotts and Ware. Further repairs and improvements were made to the cuts between Ware and Hertford in 1766-67 and 1850. Barges drawn by horses continued to reach Hertford until at least 1956, and by tug for a few years thereafter.

The Stort Navigation, involving the dredging of much of the river, the digging of several cuts, and construction of 15 locks, was rapidly constructed following the passing of the Stort Navigation Act in 1766.

In the west of the county authorisation to cut the Grand Junction Canal (Grand Union) was granted in 1793. Aldenham (Elstree) Reservoir, completed in 1797 to feed the canal, was the first genuinely large open body of water in Hertfordshire. The Grand Junction Canal, which in places utilised river courses, was completed in 1800 in which year the Aylesbury Arm was also opened. The four reservoirs at Tring were constructed between 1802-17. Wilstone Reservoir was extended in 1836 and 1839. The Wendover Arm of the canal, which still supported a diverse dragonfly community in 1986, is currently being restored for the use of leisure craft.

The turbidity of waterways used for navigation would undoubtedly have been a limitation on dragonfly populations.

Hilfield Park Reservoir, which supplies drinking water and is the only other major reservoir in the county, was filled in 1956.

Hertfordshire has no natural or semi-natural lakes or large bodies of open water. Thus the construction of lakes in large estates, mostly in the second half of the 18th century, introduced a new habitat. Most were formed by simply damming, broadening, or diverting a river or stream. These included the lakes at Brocket Park, Panshanger Park (1755), Ponsbourne Park, Tewinwater (1756), Verulamium, Woodhall Park (1777) and Wormleybury (1767). Repton's landscaping of Panshanger Park also included cutting a new course for the River Mimram upstream between Poplars Green and Tewinwater Lake. The original course of the Mimram, which passed through what is now the HMWT reserve at Tewinbury, is also still evident as a narrow stream meandering across the meadows at Archers Green.

Watercress beds were another artificial habitat created in river valleys. A few drew water directly from streams. Most were located in the valleys of the chalk streams where water was drawn from natural springs or artesian bores. Few remain in operation and two, at Cassiobury Park and Lemsford Springs, have become nature reserves. The diversity of dragonfly communities at watercress beds is generally very low.

Through the first 60 years of the 19th century, and in some places beyond, water courses, wells and many ponds were grossly polluted and the sources of outbreaks of diseases such as cholera and typhoid. Records show that the Beane, Colne, Gade, Hiz, Lea, Mimram, Stort and Ver (and presumably other rivers and watercourses) were particularly badly polluted with untreated sewage, which was widely disposed of into rivers. Parts of the Grand Union Canal are also on record as being badly polluted during this period.

The now redundant linear sewage drain or manifold ditch (known these days as Hertford Cut or Hertford Ditch) that crosses the King's Meads, Hertford, to its outfall into the Lea below Ware Lock was cut in 1855. The course from the newly built sewage farm was required by an Act of Parliament, the New River Company's Hertford Sewerage Diversion Act (1854), and built by the New River Company to ensure sewage and sewage effluent did not enter the Lea above the point at which water was drawn into the New River.

Open irrigation sewage treatment plants were constructed for most towns in the second half of the 19th century. These followed a series of public health acts passed from 1835 onwards. Some towns, however, were removed from the earlier acts and not brought under a public health act until much later, eg Hertford in 1875, at which time many smaller communities were still discharging untreated sewage into the rivers. Thus Hertfordshire's rivers, streams and other watercourses probably supported a relatively poor dragonfly fauna throughout most of the 19th century.

Managed ponds, usually lined with puddled clay, on farms, commons and village greens, were once one of the county's major biological aquatic assets. However the need to produce more home grown food, conversion of grassland to arable, and replacement of draw horses with tractors, resulted in many being lost by abandonment, neglect and natural or deliberate infill. Mostly used for watering animals, the number halved from 7,007 in 1881 to 3,595 in 1978 (Marshall 1987).

Permanent pasture and rough grazing land halved between 1933-45, and again by 1991. The biological quality and stock of remaining 'farm' ponds continue to decline, mostly as a result of neglect, pollution and development. The acid ponds on heaths, heathy commons and in the woodlands on the London Clay, eg at Bricket Wood, Broxbourne Woods, Hertford Heath and Patmore Heath, are of county importance as dragonfly habitats and need to be given high priority for management for nature conservation purposes.

By comparison, since the late 1950s, and with the availability of durable liners and fibreglass bodies, there has been a huge increase in tap- and rain-filled garden ponds. Large Red Damselflies, Azure Damselflies, Blue-tailed Damselflies, Southern Hawkers, and Broad-bodied Chasers are the main species to have colonised these habitats. Ruddy Darters have recently been found breeding in some of the more mature and less managed ponds, often in well-wooded gardens. Common Darters are regularly seen at garden ponds but their breeding status at these is unclear.

By the mid-1940s flooded gravel pits, dug to meet the demand for sand and gravel for the rapid expansion of London in the 1930s, and flooded bomb craters had provided a large number of high quality lake and new pond habitats. Early colonisers of these included Black-tailed Skimmers, which, at that time, were still uncommon in the county. Since then the continued demand for mineral has produced the extensive mosaics of lakes that now occupy much of the lower Colne and Lea valleys. Some of these now hold the richest aggregations of dragonflies to be found in the county.

After the Second World War ecologically fine and relatively extensive areas of wet floodplain grassland existed in most river valleys. Saturated in winter through to spring, and subject to seasonal flooding, they were drained by invertebrate rich dykes and ditches, which retained water throughout the year. As a result of increased water abstraction, climatic change, and other factors, water levels have been lowered, and the remaining valley grasslands have become very much drier. The swamplands that characterised parts of the floodplains 60 years ago no longer exist as such. Further recent examination of the vegetation of Hertford Meads and meadows in the Ver Valley indicate valley grasslands are becoming more acid, with possible long term implications for associated wetlands and the species composition of their dragonfly communities.

Hertfordshire's rivers (see map below) divide into two types. First are the gravel bottomed calcareous streams that originate from springs emerging from the base of the Chilterns. A few like the Hiz, Ivel, Rhee and Oughton flow northwards feeding into the Cam. Others flow southwards from the chalk crossing large areas of Boulder Clay and Clay-with-Flints. The eastern group, Ash, Rib, Beane, Quin, and Mimram, together with the Stort, feed the Lea in the east. The western group, Bulbourne, Chess, Gade and Ver, feed the Colne in the west. Most are also 'bournes' which flow in periods of high water levels in the chalk aquifers beneath.

The second types are the deeper, slower flowing, lowland rivers Colne, Lea and Stort.

Although Hertfordshire's rivers generally support less diverse dragonfly populations than the still or lentic habitats they, nonetheless, make an important contribution to the county's aquatic fauna. In particular the remaining sections of the original courses of the Lea and Stort continue to support important dragonfly populations.

Water abstraction, pollution, especially from artificial fertilisers and other agro-chemicals, and other factors such as climatic change, continue to adversely affect and significantly change Hertfordshire's rivers. Flows having ceased from many springs, the upper sections of the Gade, Ver, Mimram,

*Hertfordshire's rivers (after Dony 1967)*

Beane and Rib, have become dry, and flows in the lowland rivers are much reduced. Parts of the Lea, especially above Hertford where it has its confluence with the Mimram, Beane and Rib, and the Colne are sustained by treated sewage effluent. Low flows have allowed the accumulation of silt and caused river channels to become shallower and narrower. Indeed the biology and ecology of some of the county's rivers are beginning to resemble linear ponds.

Between 1994-97 the Hertfordshire Biological (formerly Environmental) Records Centre, in conjunction with the HMWT, carried out a countywide habitat survey. The results of this important work, known as The Hertfordshire Habitat Survey Project, are detailed in a series of ten reports, one for each of the areas administered by the county's constituent district councils. The reports, published between June 1997 and November 1998, calculated the amount of aquatic habitats in the county as shown in Table 2.

In summary the whole of Hertfordshire's land surface has been altered by human activity and endeavour. The biological quality of most of the remaining semi-natural wetlands remains poor and in urgent need of conservation measures that would reduce pollution and restore river flows. Although no substitute for semi-natural habitats, the creation of artificial habitats such as flooded mineral workings and the huge increase in garden ponds has been hugely beneficial to dragonfly populations. Thus, although the biological quality and nature of Hertfordshire's aquatic habitats at the end of the 20th century is very different from that which existed even 50 years ago, it now supports a dragonfly fauna probably richer than at any time in its post mediaeval history.

*Table 2: Aquatic habitat types in Hertfordshire*

| Habitat type and description | Area (ha) length (km) or number |
|---|---|
| **Open water.** Water lying beyond the limits of swamp or emergent vegetation. This category includes features such as ornamental lakes, reservoirs and flooded mineral extraction sites. Also recorded in this category are linear water features such as rivers, streams and canals. | 623.3 ha |
| **Swamp.** Habitat comprising emergent vegetation typical of the transition between open water and exposed land. Generally occurring in standing water for a large part of the year, swamps may also occasionally be found on substrates that are seldom immersed such as the later stages of succession to marshy grassland.<br>    Narrow strips of swamp vegetation bordering watercourses are classified as marginal vegetation. | 94.8 ha |
| **Mire, flush and spring.** Characterised by the presence of the water table at or just below the ground surface, and associated with water movement, this group comprises a complex series of habitats. | 2.1 ha |
| **Inundation.** | 4.6 ha |
| **Marginal aquatic vegetation.** This category includes all narrow strips of emergent vegetation occurring on the margins of lowland watercourses where the water table is permanently high. | 12.3 ha |
| **Total length of river, stream and canal.** | 730.85 km |
| **Total number of ponds** (not recorded as open water). | 2608 |
| **Percentage of the county area (161280.72 ha) covered by aquatic habitats.** | 0.46% |

# 4. The Atlas Project 2000-2005

## General

The term 'Atlas', in a biological recording context, can be defined as a compendium of maps illustrating the distribution of a particular taxonomic group across a defined area. In this instance the taxonomic group is dragonflies and the defined area is the administrative county of Hertfordshire.

For the purpose of this survey, recorders used the 1:25000 scale Explorer Ordnance Survey maps. Each 10km square shown on these maps was sub-divided into 25 squares, each 2km x 2km tetrads. Each tetrad was designated a letter as illustrated in the following diagram.

| E | J | P | U | Z |
|---|---|---|---|---|
| D | I | N | T | Y |
| C | H | M | S | X |
| B | G | L | R | W |
| A | F | K | Q | V |

A tetrad map of Hertfordshire is shown overleaf. Therefore, for example, in 10km square TL32, the tetrad shown shaded would have a unique identifier TL32H.

There are 458 tetrads in Hertfordshire. For those tetrads that fall on the county boundary, only those with 20% or more of Hertfordshire in the tetrad were included and only the Hertfordshire portion of the tetrad was surveyed.

It was estimated that, to cover all 458 tetrads sufficiently during the entire dragonfly flight season with the number of active recorders available, a six-year study period would be necessary. A longer period would be undesirable as it could mask trends in changes to the dragonfly distribution.

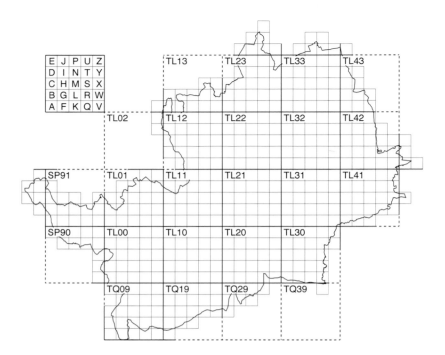

| E | J | P | U | Z |
|---|---|---|---|---|
| D | I | N | T | Y |
| C | H | M | S | X |
| B | G | L | R | W |
| A | F | K | Q | V |

*Tetrad map of*
*Hertfordshire*

## Winter planning and reconnaissance

The summer months were very busy, with recorders visiting a number of sites in each tetrad three or four times during the flight season. It was important, therefore, that the time was used efficiently and not wasted on trying to find sites, visiting sites that were unsuitable or to which there was no access. To avoid wasted journeys, much of the Atlas planning activities were actually carried during the winter months.

Once the tetrads had been allocated to members of the group, large scale Ordnance Survey maps were pored over to identify all the rivers, streams, ditches, lakes and ponds. Using a magnifying glass on these large-scale maps it was possible to locate ponds down to a diameter of only ten metres. Once the list of sites had been compiled, the sites were all visited during the winter months to assess their potential.

This exploratory work saved a considerable amount of time as many of the sites visited were dried up, overgrown, built on, polluted or not accessible. Also, many of the better sites, particularly ornamental lakes, larger garden ponds and moats were on private land. However, carrying out this reconnaissance work out of season did allow time for the owners to be identified (not always obvious) and access permission requested.

The winter planning and reconnaissance work was quite laborious but paid dividends in the knowledge that all sites visited during the summer months were accessible, suitable and likely to contribute to the Atlas Project.

## Coverage

It can prove difficult to know when an allocated tetrad has been sufficiently surveyed, so that the records produced provide a reasonably accurate reflection of the species that are present. Some county atlases are produced with a limited number of field volunteer workers. Unless the work is well planned it is easy for the field recorders to visit just sites that interest them or those that are geographically close to where they live. As a result the Atlas could be mapping the distribution of recorders, not dragonflies.

At the start of each year a number of tetrads were allocated to our small team of experienced recorders. These tetrads were visited three-four times during the dragonfly flight season to ensure that the maximum number of species was recorded. At the end of the season the results were reviewed to determine whether each tetrad had been adequately surveyed or needed more work next season. However, in addition to these planned surveys a significant number of records were received from 'casual recorders' not necessarily involved in the Atlas project and not providing systematic coverage of the tetrads they visited.

Therefore, to ensure adequate coverage of all tetrads additional criteria were needed. The method selected was the 'Indicator Species' criterion. Three resident species (including one late season species) that were known to be common and widely distributed within the county were chosen. It seemed reasonable that all tetrads with suitable water bodies should contain these species. Therefore, a tetrad could be considered as adequately covered if all three were recorded or if the recorder provided information that there was insufficient suitable habitat in a particular tetrad to support them.

## The three species indicator

The indicator species selected were as follows:

• **Common Blue Damselfly** *Enallagma cyatherigerum* or
**Azure Damselfly** *Coenagrion puella*

The Common Blue and Azure Damselflies are both common and widespread and, therefore, may be expected to be recorded in any tetrad. However, Common Blues tend to prefer the larger expanses of water, whereas Azures are quite at home in well-vegetated ponds and ditches with very little open water.

As some tetrads may not include both habitats, the first criterion was deemed to have been fulfilled if either of the species had been recorded.

• **Blue-tailed Damselfly** *Ischnura elegans*

Blue-tailed Damselflies are also widespread and common and are very catholic in their habitat preference. They are, therefore, also likely to be recorded in most tetrads and were selected as the second indicator species.

• **Common Darter** *Sympetrum striolatum*

The Common Darter was selected as the third indicator species as it is both widespread and common, but emerges later in the flight season. Therefore, apart from being expected to occur in most tetrads, it is also a good indicator of whether the tetrad has been visited in the middle-latter part of the flight season.

Although these species are common and it is often possible to observe all three on a single visit, we were aware that the Common Darter is more often seen later in the season. Therefore, in order to see all three, more than one visit to the tetrad was likely to be needed. As the majority of the records received included dates and site names it was also possible to ascertain from the records how often the tetrad had been visited and whether or not a selection of sites within the tetrad had been surveyed. Combining all these factors we were able to judge when any given tetrad had received adequate coverage.

Clearly the census work on flying insects could only be carried out during the summer months. However, it was possible to visit some of the more barren tetrads during the winter months, to confirm that there was no suitable dragonfly habitat, and that further visits during the flight season would not be worthwhile. In this way these tetrads could be regarded as 'poor, but covered' without wasting valuable recording time during the summer months.

Although the number of recorders did vary slightly during the study, all 458 tetrads were covered during the 6-year period. Of these, 299 (65.3%) achieved the three-species indicator criterion. The remaining 159 tetrads had not achieved the three-species criterion at the end of the study despite focussed survey work and were designated 'poor but covered'.

The three-species criterion is a good coverage indicator and also provides an indication of those tetrads having reasonable dragonfly habitat. A map of those tetrads where the three-species indicator was achieved is shown opposite. The map shows that in the central, southern and eastern regions of the county, most tetrads have suitable dragonfly habitat. However, in the western and northern regions, there are a number of areas where the three-species indicator was not achieved, indicating a lack of suitable habitat.

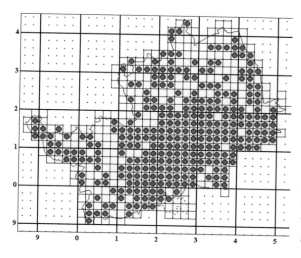

*Tetrads where the three-species indicator was achieved*

The main reason for these tetrads failing to achieve the three-species indicator was a combination of the following factors:

a. The inclusion of vast areas of arable farm land

b. A general lack of streams, rivers, ponds and lakes and any other suitable water bodies. In many cases, the only sources of water were field drainage ditches, which were fast flowing during the winter months and dry during the summer.

Only a few tetrads failed to achieve the three-species criteria due to the inclusion of built up areas, which seems to indicate that towns are richer in suitable dragonfly habitat than large expanses of arable farmland. This may be due to towns having areas of wasteland or parkland with areas of water, or even numerous garden ponds.

## Records and recorders

Over the six-year period of the study, from 2000-05 inclusive, a total of 14,671 records were received from 119 recorders. The recorders submitting 500 or more records were as follows:

| | |
|---|---|
| Denis Shepperson | 2196 |
| Alan Reynolds | 1915 |
| Barry Reed | 1737 |
| Denis Shepperson and Christine Shepperson | 1333 |
| Steve Murray | 1287 |
| Christine Shepperson | 722 |
| Arthur Smith | 506 |

A full list of recorders in alphabetical order is given in Chapter 1 and we should extend our thanks to all of them, as without their input this Atlas would not have been possible.

# 5. The occurrence and distribution of dragonflies in Hertfordshire

## Introduction

Although there have been numerous articles published in various journals dating back to the early 1900s about the status of dragonflies and damselflies in Hertfordshire, it has not been possible to provide an authoritative statement on their distribution across the county. The production of this Atlas will therefore provide a snapshot in time representing the status of our current knowledge. It is hoped that naturalists will be able to build on this and compare the current distribution with that sometime in the future.

The following sections present the results for each of 19 regularly recorded species covering:

- Identification
- Confusion species
- Behaviour
- Flight period
- Historical records
- Distribution in the county

The historical records are included as an indication of the status of the various species at the time. However, it should be noted that there were fewer recorders sending in records and no previous survey has been carried out. It would therefore be unwise to extrapolate any firm distribution trends from the historical literature records.

# Banded Demoiselle

*Calopteryx splendens* (Harris 1782)

*Banded Demoiselle*

The stunning appearance of the male Banded Demoiselle must make it one of the most distinctive and easily identified dragonflies in Hertfordshire. The thorax and abdomen are a vivid metallic blue with large blue-black 'bands' on each wing, which are very conspicuous both when settled and in flight. The female is a metallic green with greenish wings. Although classified as a damselfly both sexes are much larger than all the other damselfly species in the county.

Banded Demoiselles are generally found close to running water although wanderers can often been seen well away from water. As with all other dragonflies and damselflies, they always return to water to breed.

In their breeding habitat, they are frequently seen perched on vegetation overhanging the water. Periodically, they will take off for a characteristic jerky up and down flight that resembles butterflies. On warm calm days, many can be seen 'dancing' during their display flights. Males have often been observed chasing a female as she arrives at the water.

The main confusion species is the Beautiful Demoiselle, which has not been recorded recently in the county. However, the more likely confusion species for the female Banded Demoiselle is the Emerald Damselfly. Both are predominantly green and confusing a female Banded Demoiselle with an Emerald Damselfly is a common mistake amongst beginners. However, the wings of a female Banded Demoiselle are green, are much larger than those of a damselfly and are held along the body when at rest. The wings of an Emerald Damselfly are clear and are normally held at 45° to the body.

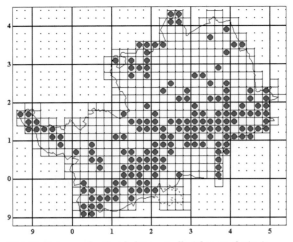

*Distribution map for Banded Demoiselle (2km resolution)*

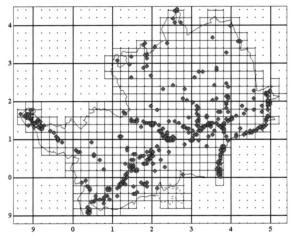

*Distribution map for Banded Demoiselle (0.5km resolution)*

The flight season may start as early as the middle of April and last until the first week of October, although the main season is from the second week in May until the middle of September.

Historically the species may have been less widespread in its distribution than it is today as Palmer in 1940 described it as 'one of our most beautiful British dragonflies, but... very local in Hertfordshire'. He says, 'I have seen it, though rarely, at Oughton Head, near Hitchin. It is more abundant in the Welwyn district along the rivers Mimram and Lea, and by the Lea between Hertford and Broxbourne. It is also found along the Colne near Aldenham and Watford. Bertram Lloyd says it does not occur in the Elstree district.' (Palmer 1940).

The Atlas 2km distribution map shows that the Banded Demoiselle was present in 171 tetrads (37%) and more widespread than suggested by Palmer (1940).

The map does not show any obvious pattern in the distribution of the species, but if the map is reproduced with a resolution of 0.5km instead of the 2km tetrad, then it can be seen that the majority of the records are closely correlated with the county's streams and rivers.

## Emerald Damselfly

*Lestes sponsa* (Hansemann 1823)

The Emerald Damselfly is generally associated with still water, particularly shallow ponds with dense stands of emergent vegetation. They spend a considerable amount of time settled, frequently hanging vertically from a reed stem. Their flight usually lasts for only a few seconds before they settle again.

Males are metallic green with blue pruinescence on parts of the thorax

between the wings, and on abdominal segments one, two, eight and nine. They have blue eyes. Females are a dark emerald green with no pruinescence.

One of the key distinguishing features that separates this species from the other Hertfordshire damselfly species is the way the wings are held at 45° when at rest. Damselflies normally fold their wings along the body when settled on vegetation. This is a very conspicuous feature and, with binoculars, can be seen from distances up to 30m.

The flight season may start as early as the beginning of June and last until the third week of September, although the main season is from the middle of June until the end of August.

There is little reference to this species in the early *Trans Herts NHS*. A small breeding colony was reported at Park Street in 1952 (Lloyd 1954). They were seen at Wilstone, Little Tring and Hertford Heath in 1955, also abundant around rush-fringed ponds on Patmore Heath in the same year (Lloyd, 1958). Bryan Sage reported the species on the River Colne at Old Parkbury in his 1966 report (Sage 1966) and said they were seen at Smallford Pit in 1970-71 and Rickmansworth Pits in 1972.

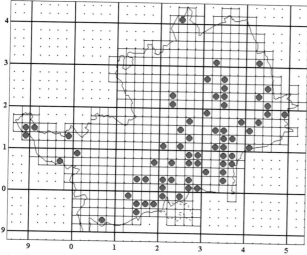

*Distribution map for Emerald Damselfly*

The Atlas distribution map shows that, whilst the species is fairly well represented in the county, it is concentrated in the south, east and extreme west of the county. It is certainly not common, being found in only 67 of the 458 tetrads (15%), although is probably now more widespread than reported in the 1950-70s.

## White-legged Damselfly
*Platycnemis pennipes* (Pallas 1771)

*White-legged Damselfly*

The White-legged Damselfly is the least widespread and rarest dragonfly in Hertfordshire. In the 1990s, prior to the Atlas Project, it was only recorded in one tetrad, TL30Q, at Marsh Bridge in Cheshunt.

Males are a paler blue than other blue damselfly species with distinctive linear abdominal markings. The prominent feature is the white legs that are broad, flattened and 'feathered'. These are characteristically left dangling in flight especially when males are in the presence of females. Females mature from a very pale '*lactea*' phase through to a light green. Tenerals are very pale fawny-pink.

The main confusion species is the Common Blue Damselfly where the tenerals have pale abdomens and legs.

White-legged Damselflies favour rivers and canals with lush bankside vegetation. They can often be found in meadows adjacent to their breeding sites.

Their flight season extends from the end of May until the middle of August.

In the 1945 *Trans Herts NHS* two records of White-legged Damselfly are reported. The first is along the Lee Canal near Wormley from Mr and Mrs Hayward (Hayward & Hayward 1945). 'In 1942 we saw one male by the canal on 27th June, one on 12th July and three – all by a stretch of about ten yards of the bank – on 19th July. These were all about half a mile south of King's Weir and were in Hertfordshire, except for that seen on 12th July, which was just over the Essex border. This is the second known locality for the species in Herts, the first being the Tring colony discovered by Bertram Lloyd in the same year.'

After the death of her husband in 1944, Sylvia Lloyd continued to report on the Tring colony (Lloyd, 1948). She reported that in 1945 there were, 'several individuals among the males of this species of the white [female] variety, known as *lactea*, in the little colony at the Tring station canal. They stood out quite strikingly among the normal pale blue insects.' In 1949 she found a new site in the Tring area (Lloyd 1952). 'On 27th July 1949, I saw a mating pair by the canal near Marsworth, a new station for this species.'

By 1950 there is a hint that all is not well with the colony at Tring, when she notes (Lloyd 1953), that only a few were seen where, 'until recently there was a considerable colony'. However there is news of another site when a field meeting of the HNHS sees the species near Watford.

On 1st July 1951, the HNHS saw a good many by the canal in Cassiobury Park; several mating pairs were closely examined. One mating pair was seen by the Old Aylesbury Canal. In 1952 she reports a new site, also near Watford (Lloyd 1954), 'on 14th August in the Grove, near Watford, I caught a mating pair in a glass topped box.'

Signs that the west Herts colonies were having difficulties reappears in S Hodgson's report (Hodgson 1959). Although he finds the White-legged Damselfly to be, 'generally fairly common on GUC [Grand Union Canal] between Tring station and Bulbourne' he also says that, 'the small colony on the Aylesbury Canal near Marsworth found by Bertram Lloyd has apparently not been observed since 1952.'

Sylvia Lloyd's report on the dragonflies seen in 1960 carries a similar message, contributed by S Hodgson (Lloyd 1961). Only one White-legged Damselfly was seen by the Halton Canal and they were very scarce in Tring canal cutting. 'The canal is now gradually coming into use again for pleasure boats, and possibly changes in its present rich dragonfly fauna may eventually take place... owing to increasing traffic and consequent water pollution the future of this colony is very doubtful.'

Her record from the following year (Lloyd 1963), when they were, 'fairly plentiful in canal cutting near Bulbourne', is the last until B Sage reports a sighting in 1969 (Sage 1970). He then says, 'recorded in the Tring canal cutting and in Cassiobury Park... The record from the Tring canal cutting is the first

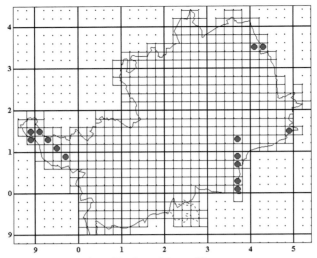

*Distribution map for White-legged Damselfly*

from this long established locality since 1961'. Also in 1969, Tom Gladwin caught a female by the River Mimram at Tewinbury.

In 1995 Tom Gladwin reported that the species, 'seems to have declined in the lower Lea valley', and in his 1997 report he says, 'of the seventeen resident species (in Herts) only one, the White-legged Damselfly… seems to be in overall decline.'

The White-legged Damselfly was recorded in 14 tetrads (3%) during the Atlas survey, compared to just one during the 1990s.

The habitat requirements of the White-legged Damselfly are not fully understood as they can be present in one area and absent in another where, on face value, the habitats appear to be similar. Although scarce in Hertfordshire, they are relatively common in Bedfordshire, Buckinghamshire and Essex.

As there are few records for this species in Hertfordshire, it is worth recording the tetrads where they were recorded for future reference:

| Tetrad | Location |
| --- | --- |
| SP81W | Grand Union Canal (GUC) Aylesbury Arm South of Puttenham |
| SP81X | GUC Aylesbury Arm West of Wilstone |
| SP81X | Millhoppers Pasture |
| SP91C | GUC Aylesbury Arm Wilstone |
| SP91G | GUC Wendover Arm North |
| SP91K | GUC New Ground – Cow Roast Lock |
| SP90U | GUC South of Lock 47 – Dudswell |
| TL30Q | Marsh Bridge Cheshunt |
| TL30Q | Bowyers Water Cheshunt |
| TL30R | Thistly Marsh Cheshunt |
| TL30T | Silvermeade Broxbourne |
| TL30U | Admirals Walk Hoddesdon |
| TL31R | River Ash Amwell Quarry |
| TL43C | New Lake West * |
| TL43H | New Lake East* |
| TL41X | River Stort Navigation Sawbridgeworth |

* Please note that New Lake is a private fishing lake.

# Large Red Damselfly

*Pyrrhosoma nymphula* (Sulzer 1776)

*Large Red Damselfly*

The Large Red Damselfly is one of the most well known species, being the first to emerge in the season and is the only red damselfly in the county. The male is predominantly red with black marking towards the hind end of the abdomen. The females are somewhat more variable having differing degrees of black and red. However, the black markings on the females are almost invariably more extensive than those on the males.

The only confusion species based on body colour might be the Common and Ruddy Darters. Although the colouration is the same, the darters are far more robust, hold their wings forward when perched and are fast strong fliers. There really should not be any difficulty in separating the damselfly from the darters.

The Large Red is usually encountered perched on lake or pond side vegetation but also favours shrubs and bushes close to water. Although they are usually found in relatively small numbers, it is possible to find colonies with up to 500 insects present.

The flight season runs from the middle of April until the end of July, although a few insects can continue until the third week of August.

Palmer (1930) considered this damselfly, 'comparatively scarce and local in the north of the county... at Knebworth Lake in very small numbers. In the St Albans and Watford districts it seems much commoner.' B Lloyd finds it only rather 'scantily' present at Hilfield (Lloyd 1937).

Sylvia Lloyd reported in the 1952 *Trans Herts NHS*, 'On 27th July 1949, I saw two individuals of the handsome bright red *Pyrrhosoma nymphula* by

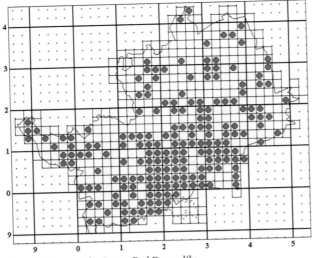

*Distribution map for Large Red Damselfly*

the lily pond at Wall Hall.' She also reported it by the Aylesbury Canal that year where, in 1959, she noted, (Lloyd, 1961) 'a few paired and ovipositing in the clay pits... on 16th May.' In 1959 they were also seen at Ball's Wood and Smallford Pits.

During the 1950s and 1960s they were seen at several sites including Hertford Heath, Patmore Heath, Broxbourne Wood and Bramfield Forest. In the 1970s B Sage writes of sightings that include Cassiobury Park, the River Beane at Waterford and the River Mimram at Panshanger.

The Atlas distribution map shows that the Large Red Damselfly is one of our commonest damselflies and is distributed throughout the county, being recorded in 188 tetrads (41%).

The highest concentration of records is in the south of the county, with fewer in the east where many other species are recorded. This may reflect the lack of suitable ponds and lakes in this part of the county.

## Red-eyed Damselfly
*Erythromma najas* (Hansemann 1823)

The Red-eyed Damselfly is a most striking insect. At first glance, the male with its dark abdomen and blue colouration on segments nine and ten resembles the Blue-tailed Damselfly, although the Red-eyed Damselfly is more robust and has crimson red eyes. The females have duller eyes and lack the blue on segments nine and ten.

It is a fast and powerful flier and is normally seen either dashing around low over the water frequently in combat with Common Blue Damselflies vying for control of the floating vegetation. It will also settle for long periods on floating vegetation such as water lily leaves, where it waits for any passing female. Like the Common Blue Damselfly, it favours the larger ponds, lakes and canals.

Apart from the Blue-tailed Damselfly mentioned above, the only confusion species is the Small Red-eyed Damselfly, *Erythromma viridulum*, which was first recorded in the UK as recently as 1999. The Small Red-eyed Damselfly is smaller, with tomato-red coloured eyes and blue wedges on the underside of segments three and eight.

The flight season starts in early May and runs through to the middle of September.

Palmer (1930) wrote that the Red-eyed Damselfly was 'a very local insect of retiring habits and only a recent addition to the county list. In June 1927, I took three specimens, a male and two females along the River Colne near Aldenham. It probably occurs in other localities and only needs looking for'.

Hodgson (1959) reported, that he had obtained additional Herts localities for certain species from the well-known dragonfly author Cynthia Longfield. For *E. najas* she contributed a record from E R Speyer who had considered the species common in the Hoddesdon district. No date was given for the Speyer record.

Bertram Lloyd also found this species to be very local in its distribution (Lloyd 1937) and reported, 'though I have searched carefully, I have found this species nowhere in the district except at the Lily Pool near Aldenham. On 9th June 1937, I found a single male, and on 13th June saw three males there with

*Red-eyed Damselfly*

a single female and an immature individual – all among rough herbage at the waters edge.'

He mentions Ray Palmer's earlier record and comments, 'this may well have been close to the Lily Pool which, however, being a kind of backwater of the River Colne, sluiced (with hatches) and not properly speaking flowing water, would be a more suitable breeding station for this species. The males, at least,... show a predilection for perching on leaves lying flat on the surface of the water... in contrast to other *Agrionidae*'.

By 1940 Palmer still only found this damselfly to be 'a very local species, which seems to have been found only in one locality in the county' (Palmer

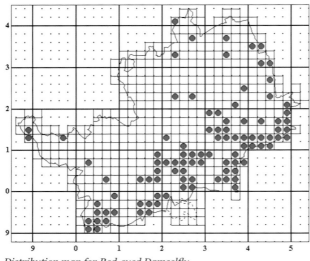

*Distribution map for Red-eyed Damselfly*

1940). He comments, 'the small area to which this species seems to be confined is remarkable'.

But in 1942 B Lloyd found them at another site. 'On 3rd July 1942, I discovered a small colony... near Wilstone, on the Aylesbury branch of the Grand Union Canal, by the Buckinghamshire border. Several unattached males... a few pairs were engaged in oviposition, using for this purpose the leaves of *Potamogeton perfoliatus*, which grows lushly at this spot' (Lloyd 1944). The following year Mr and Mrs Hayward (Hayward & Hayward 1945) found a strong and compact colony on the canal near Cheshunt on 12th June.

In the 1950s further sites were reported including, 'in considerable numbers on Cheshunt marshes on 7th June 1952 by B Sage.' (Lloyd 1954) and 'several... River Lea, Amwell, on 26th June, 1956.' (Lloyd 1958). In the 1960s there were records from Bourne End Gravel Pits and Nyn Park, Northaw (Sage 1966).

The Red-eyed Damselfly is generally associated with the larger expanses of water, which is reflected in the distribution map by the concentration of records in the south and east of the county. The Red-eyed Damselfly was recorded in 97 tetrads (21%), which would suggest a considerable increase compared to the mid 1900s as described above.

## Small Red-eyed Damselfly
*Erythromma viridulum* (Charpentier 1840)

The Small Red-eyed Damselfly is, as the name suggests, a smaller member of the same genus as the Red-eyed Damselfly. It is very similar in appearance to the Red-eyed but, apart from the slightly smaller size, has tomato-red coloured eyes and blue wedges on the underside of segments three and eight. The only other possible confusion species is the Blue-tailed Damselfly, which lacks red eyes.

Like the Red-eyed Damselfly, the Small Red-eyed Damselfly prefers well-vegetated still water habitat. It especially favours pools with an abundance of submerged aquatic plants such as Milfoil, Hornwort and Canadian Pondweed.

The flight season starts from the last week in June, although the main period is from the end of July until early September. It is quite likely that the season will become earlier when the species becomes more established and less reliant on migrants.

The Small Red-eyed Damselfly was first discovered in the UK at three sites in Essex in July 1999. It then continued to spread into English counties at an incredible rate and at the time of publication of this Atlas has expanded across most of southern England. During the early colonisation phase Hertfordshire was bordered by several areas that had colonies of the newcomer, but none within the county.

The first Small Red-eyed Damselfly for Hertfordshire was recorded by Graham White. In the October 2001 edition of *Brachytron*, he wrote:

'I had been carrying out a breeding bird survey of the Cheshunt gravel pits area throughout the summer and in the quieter moments checking through the Red-eyes in several areas. On my last visit (24th August) around midday I wandered over to Bowyers Gravel Pit to pick up any late grebe or duck broods.

As it was a good sunny day the lake was heaving with *Odonata*. Red-eyed Damselflies *Erythromma najas* were abundant along the western side where there were lily patches and other areas of aquatic vegetation breaking the

*Small Red-eyed Damselfly*

water's surface. I checked through around 40-50 Red-eyed before spotting what I suspected to be a male Small Red-eyed *Erythromma viridulum* on a lily leaf towards the northern end of the lake.

The Small Red-eyed was watched repeatedly flying and returning to the same perch for about ten minutes, confirming identification. At one time it came slightly closer to the bank and a photo was obtained. I moved on around the lake, still checking, but found no others.

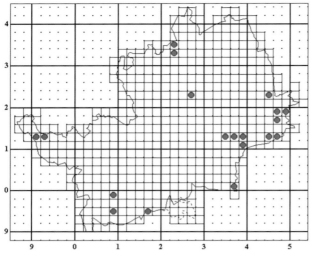

*Distribution map for Small Red-eyed Damselfly*

To me, the key features of Small Red-eyed are the apparent sloping divide of blue under black on the end of the abdomen (caused by the blue wedge on the side of segment eight) and general size and jizz, together with the interactions with Red-eyed.'

By the end of the Atlas Project the Small Red-eyed Damselfly had been recorded in 19 tetrads (4%) across the county. However, this cannot be regarded as a true indication of the status of the species in the county over the Atlas period, as many of the 458 tetrads would have already been surveyed before the Small Red-eyed started to colonise, and would not have been revisited.

## Azure Damselfly

*Coenagrion puella* (Linnaeus 1758)

Although the Azure Damselfly is one of our commonest damselflies, it is also one that causes the most confusion amongst the less experienced dragonfly enthusiasts due to its similarity to the Common Blue Damselfly.

The males of both species are bright turquoise blue with black markings on the thorax and the abdomen. However, at close range, the male Azure Damselfly can be identified by the 'horseshoe' or 'Honda sign' on segment two, and the fact that only half of segment nine is blue. The Common Blue Damselfly, however, has a 'lollipop' on segment two, the whole of segment nine is blue and the antehumeral stripes are usually much broader. Older females of both species are much drabber than the males and may be variable in colouration. Detailed descriptions can be found in any good field guide.

The Azure Damselfly tends to be found in smaller ponds or larger water bodies in those sections that are well vegetated, streams and ditches, whereas the Common Blue Damselfly prefers the larger expanses of open water. The Common Blue is more robust and spends more of its time flying low over the water, often in combat with Red-eyed Damselflies, fighting for control of the lily pads.

The flight season is long, from the end of April to the middle of September.

*Azure Damselfly*     Palmer (1930) reported, 'This is one of the commonest species, and I have found it in all suitable localities that I have investigated, sometimes occurring in great numbers'. Early observers tend to call the *Zygoptera* (or damselflies), 'Needle dragonflies' and B Lloyd refers to this species as the 'Common Blue Needle Dragonfly' (Lloyd 1937).

The words commonly used to describe it in the *HNHS Transactions* are 'abundant', 'numerous', 'plentiful' and present in 'myriads' which consistently affirm its status.

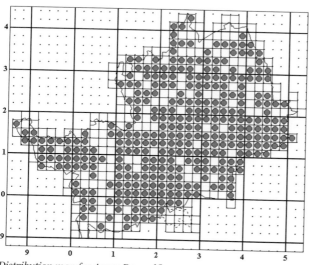

The Azure Damselfly is both common and widespread. It was recorded in 319 tetrads (70%), which together with the Blue-tailed Damselfly (71%), is the highest number of tetrads recorded for all the Hertfordshire species of dragonfly and damselfly.

*Distribution map for Azure Damselfly*

# Common Blue Damselfly

*Enallagma cyathigerum* (Charpentier 1840)

*Common Blue
Damselfly*

The Common Blue Damselfly is both common and widespread and is probably one of our most well known damselflies. In suitable habitats, such as large open ponds and lakes, hundreds and even thousands can be seen flying over floating vegetation and seemingly open water. Careful observation will reveal submerged vegetation below, where females will be ovipositing. In such conditions it can often be seen swarming over the water's surface. This behaviour distinguishes it from the closely related Azure Damselfly.

As stated previously, the Common Blue Damselfly can be confused with the Azure Damselfly, as at long range the males, being predominantly turquoise blue and black, are very similar. However, when viewed at close range or through binoculars, the male Common Blue can be identified by the broad blue antehumeral stripes, the 'lollipop' on segment two and the all blue segment nine. Whereas the male Azure Damselfly, has a 'horseshoe' or 'Honda sign' on segment two and only half of segment nine is blue. In addition, the Common Blue Damselfly is more robust and is a much stronger flier. However the best distinguishing feature when viewed side on, is the lack of the two short black stripes on the side of the thorax that are present on Azure Damselflies.

The flight season can start as early as the end of April, but the main emergence does not occur until the second week in May. The main season finishes in the third week of September although, depending on the weather, some individuals can remain on the wing until the end of October.

Like the Azure Damselfly this species is 'Very common everywhere, and quite the dominant species in some localities' (Palmer 1930) and 'One of the commonest of the little blue needle-dragonflies' (Palmer 1940).

Lucas describes its typical habitat as, 'ponds, canals, lakes, and streams, where the surface of the water is not too much hidden by water-weeds, appear to be the favourite haunts of this delicately coloured little dragonfly. Here amongst the rushes and long grass near the banks, or often if the sun is shining, over the surface of the open water, they may sometimes be seen in swarms.' (Lucas 1900).

B Lloyd (Lloyd 1937) recorded it at Elstree (Aldenham) Reservoir and wrote, 'This lovely topaz-hued little dragonfly may be seen by the smaller reservoir in hundreds, flying among and perching inconspicuously on the rushes, water plantain, and other herbage by the waters edge, or flitting low over the surface of the pool.' His wife Sylvia Lloyd said they were 'flitting like wisps of blue' (Lloyd 1954).

In 1959, while discussing Tring Reservoirs, Hodgson commented on the Common Blue Damselfly that, 'Its seeming preference for open water (mentioned by several authors) is strange; at the reservoirs it almost invariably keeps to the shallow margins – even on a calm day – where weed and flies are plentiful' (Hodgson 1959).

This species is both common and widespread, being recorded in 267 tetrads (58%). Records are more concentrated in the south and east of the county and also at Tring Reservoirs where there are a lot of large areas of open water.

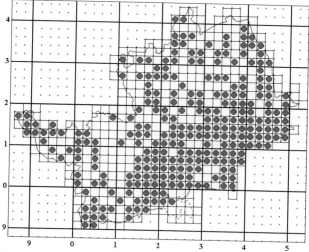

*Distribution map for Common Blue Damselfly*

# Blue-tailed Damselfly
*Ischnura elegans* (Vander Linden 1820)

The Blue-tailed Damselfly is the smallest of Hertfordshire's dragonflies. It has a very widespread distribution, as it is fairly catholic in its habitat requirements. It is reputed to be reasonably tolerant of pollution. Although rarely seen in large numbers, it can normally be found in any insignificant ditch or pond and also in streams, rivers and lakes.

As the name suggests, the male Blue-tailed Damselfly is easily identifiable by its very conspicuous blue tail on segment eight, which shows up well in contrast to the black abdomen.

*Male Blue-tailed Damselfly*

*Female Blue-tailed Damselfly* 'rufescens' *form*

*Female Blue-tailed Damselfly* 'violacea' *form*

For the females the situation is more complex. All females start out as either the '*rufescens*' form where the thorax is a rufous colour or the '*violacea*' form where the thorax is violet. As the '*rufescens*' females mature the thorax and segment eight turn brown. This mature form is known as '*infuscans-obsoleta*'. The form '*violacea*' can either mature into the same colouration as their male counterparts or into the form '*infuscans*' where the thorax turns brown with black stripes and segment eight becomes brown.

The confusion species are the Red-eyed and Small Red-eyed Damselflies, as all three species can frequently be seen settled on floating vegetation such as algae and lily pads. Separating the species is fairly straightforward since, as their name suggests, both Red-eyed and Small Red-eyed Damselflies have red eyes, whereas the eyes of the Blue-tailed Damselfly are dark.

The flight season runs from the beginning of May until the middle of September, although they may be seen in late April and early October.

The Blue-tailed Damselfly can adapt to all habitat types and is both common and widespread. It was recorded in 326 tetrads (71%) which, alongside the Azure Damselfly (70%), is the highest number of tetrads of all the Hertfordshire species of dragonfly and damselfly.

*Distribution map for Blue-tailed Damselfly*

## Migrant Hawker
*Aeshna mixta* (Latreille 1805)

The Migrant Hawker is one of our latest fliers, normally not emerging until the last week in July and flying well into October. It is often seen well away from water patrolling woodland rides and is sometimes recorded in large numbers.

The Migrant Hawker is medium sized, being only 80% the size of an Emperor. The male has blue eyes, a brown thorax with minimal antehumeral stripes and a dark abdomen with a pair of blue spots on each segment. There is also a yellow 'golf tee' and a blue band on segment two. The blue band is distinctive and can easily be seen in flight. The female has brown eyes with yellow spots on the abdomen.

*Migrant Hawker*     The main confusion species are the Common Hawker and the Southern Hawker. The Common Hawker is a larger insect, lacks the 'golf tee' on segment two and is not found in Hertfordshire. The Southern Hawker is also much larger, being the same size as an Emperor and both sexes have broad distinctive antehumeral stripes.

The flight season may start as early as the second week in July and last until the first week of November, although the main season is from the fourth week in July until the third week of October.

This species is now fairly common and widespread but this was not always the case. Apart from an old 19th century record, it appears to have been unrecorded in Herts, until it was found in 1936 at Elstree Reservoir (Palmer, 1940).

Lucas commented, '...the species is undoubtedly scarce' and goes on to say that it seems '...to be almost confined to the south-eastern corner of England and the Channel Islands, and even there but few captures have ever been recorded' (Lucas 1900).

In 1940 Palmer described it as an uncommon species. After that it seems to have spread or recorders became more vigilant in looking for them.

B Lloyd reported that he discovered 'two thriving colonies' of this 'rather rare species' that were apparently well established, at Tring Reservoirs (Marsworth and Wilstone) on the Bucks border. He saw it on the wing as late as 20th October 1941 (Lloyd 1944). H H S and M G Hayward, in their article,

*Dragonflies of the Lea Canal* (Hayward & Hayward 1945) reported it between Cheshunt and Wormley in 1942 and 1943.

Hodgson mentions further sites, 'seen most years in fluctuating but generally small numbers at Tring Reservoirs, and since 1950 on the Aylesbury Canal with two on the Halton Canal in 1953' (Hodgson 1959).

The first definite evidence of breeding came at Wilstone Reservoir in 1955 (Hodgson, 1959). During the 1950s and 60s it was reported more regularly, although still referred to by S Lloyd in 1960 as the Scarce Aeshna.

B Lloyd (1938) describes it as, 'much addicted to hovering kestrel-wise when hunting.' He also says 'it hunts for food very late in the day and in rainy and overcast weather... when on the wing, it will often shoot up vertically after a fly – with a kind of upward stoop of three or four feet – with wonderful ease and force of wing and muscle'.

Today the Migrant Hawker is both common and widespread in Hertfordshire, apart from the large areas of farmland around Hemel Hempstead and in the north of the county. It was recorded in 235 tetrads (51%).

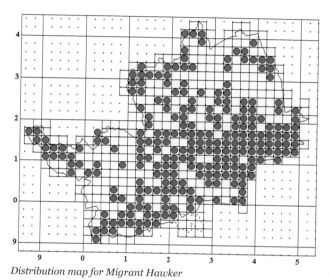

*Distribution map for Migrant Hawker*

## Southern Hawker

*Aeshna cyanea* (Müller, 1764)

The Southern Hawker is our largest late flying hawker, being the same size as the Emperor Dragonfly. It is frequently associated with woodland ponds, but is equally at home in urban habitats such as park and garden ponds. The Southern Hawker is very inquisitive and will frequently hover in front of you no more than one metre away.

The male has blue eyes, a dark thorax with wide conspicuous antehumeral stripes and a dark abdomen with green spots on each segment. The spots on segment eight are blue and, on segments nine and ten, the spots are blue and fused into a stripe. The sides of the abdomen are also blue. Females have brown eyes and a dark brown abdomen with green spots on all segments, those on segments nine and ten fused into a stripe.

The main confusion species is the Migrant Hawker. However, the Migrant Hawker is smaller, being only 80% the size of the Southern Hawker. Also the Migrant Hawker has minimal antehumeral stripes compared to the broad stripes of the Southern Hawker, and a yellow 'golf tee' and a blue band on segment two.

The flight season may start as early as the beginning of June and last until the first week of November, although the main season is from the fourth week of June until the middle of October.

Various recorders earlier this century found the Southern Hawker to be quite common. Palmer (1930) called it the commonest large dragonfly in the county and says that in some seasons it is very abundant.

Sylvia Lloyd (1953) reported 'This species remains one of the most widespread in the county. Frequently seen hawking along insect laden hedges in lanes far away from any water'.

This view of its frequent sightings away from water echoes Lucas who says, 'Though sometimes seen flying over the water... this insect is oftener met with along hedgerows and lanes, where it sometimes for a long time flies backwards and forwards over a very restricted

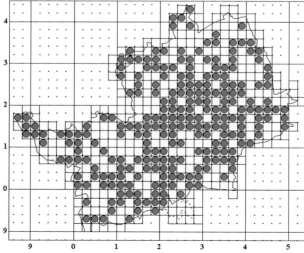

*Distribution map for Southern Hawker*

range... [it has a] rapid, powerful flight... once startled, however, it usually soars away out of sight...' (Lucas, 1900).

Bertram Lloyd calls it the Common Green-spotted Dragonfly and says that it is known to fly very late in the season. He recalls seeing one on 12th October 1935 on, 'a very cold day, one was hawking over the reeds in a wind screened corner of Elstree Reservoir.' He reports that Lucas gives it an even later record, 24th October 1897 (Lloyd 1937).

The Southern Hawker is still both common and widespread today, being recorded in 240 tetrads (52%).

## Brown Hawker

*Aeshna grandis* (Linnaeus 1758)

*Brown Hawker*

The Brown Hawker is one of the easiest dragonflies to identify, being large, brown and having cinnamon coloured wings. There is a small amount of blue along the side of the abdomen. Both sexes are similar.

As the Brown Hawker is the only dragonfly to have cinnamon coloured wings, there are no confusion species.

It is a familiar sight during the summer months patrolling up and down streams, rivers and canals, but is equally at home hunting over grassy meadows.

The flight season may start as early as the fourth week in May and last until the first week of October, although the main season is from the third week of June until the end of September.

The Brown Hawker is one of the four Hertfordshire dragonflies for which published records occur from quite early in the 19th century (Stephens 1835), the others being Migrant Hawker, Emperor Dragonfly and the Hairy Dragonfly.

In 1930 Palmer reported, 'This magnificent insect does not occur in the north of the county'. However it has been recorded in North Herts over recent years, although it is rare in the intensively farmed northeast, as are many other dragonflies.

B Lloyd said that the Brown Hawker was common in the south of the county and refered to it as the 'Great Brown Dragonfly'. He describes watching a female egg laying at Elstree Reservoir in August 1935. 'This she accomplished by pitching on pieces of flattish floating wood, or on a broken piece of branch near the pool's margin and then curving her long abdomen sickle-wise and dipping the end through the surface film of the water... it was very rapidly completed once she had fairly settled down on the chosen piece of wood' (Lloyd 1937).

S Lloyd wrote thus about the Brown Hawker, 'This handsome and powerful flier is very numerous in our county, and will often be seen when no other species is about, even in unfavourable weather. In strong sunlight it has the appearance of burnished copper, and in its dashing flight will almost touch the human observer' (Lloyd 1953).

Lucas considered it to be, '...perhaps even more powerful on the wing than *A. cyanea* and oftener seen near water, its habits are very similar to that species... and continues its evolutions till quite late in the evening, as has often been recorded.' (He mentions an instance when it was still flying when it was nearly dark). He goes on to say, '...it is voracious and fearless, and often preys on quite large insects'.

The Brown Hawker is still both common and widespread today, although more concentrated in the south and east of the county. It was recorded in 238 tetrads (52%).

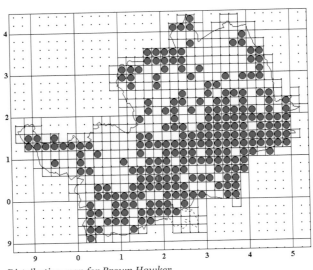

*Distribution map for Brown Hawker*

# Emperor Dragonfly

*Anax imperator* (Leach 1815)

*Emperor Dragonfly*

The Emperor Dragonfly is surely one of the best known of our dragonflies and, to many, signals the arrival of summer. No one could fail to notice this magnificent large bright blue dragonfly as it patrols endlessly up and down streams, rivers, canals and lakes. The repeated, measured pace of the flight is interrupted occasionally when the insect spirals skywards to catch an insect, before returning to its beat. A most voracious predator, the Emperor will catch and devour butterflies and damselflies as well as small insects.

The greenish blue females appear to be most confiding as, blissfully unaware of your presence, they go about the business of laying their eggs on the undersides of floating vegetation just a few metres from you.

The Emperor Dragonfly is one of our largest dragonflies. The males have green eyes, a green thorax and a bright blue abdomen with a black spine running down the upper side. The females are similar but have a greener abdomen, although this can take on a bluish hue as the insect matures.

The main confusion species are the other large Hawkers. All of these have a pair of spots on each segment of the abdomen, whereas the abdomen of the Emperor is solid blue with a black median stripe. Also, the Migrant Hawker is much smaller than the Emperor. The Common Hawker is not found in Hertfordshire.

The flight season may start as early as the second week of May and last until the second week of September, although the main season is from the beginning of June until the third week of August.

S Lloyd paints a vivid picture of a sighting in 1946, 'he showed up grandly in the fierce sunlight, literally scintillating as he hung with vibrating wings over the water.' (Lloyd 1948). The Emperor is not always easy to observe closely as it is very active and can patrol over open water for long periods without 'hanging up' on surrounding vegetation.

In the early 20th century it was regarded as rare in Herts, with Palmer (1930) reporting 'it is scarce... in June 1922, I captured a pair at Knebworth Lake, but have not met with it since.' In 1940 he said that since his 1922 sighting it had been seen in the Hitchin neighbourhood, 'but it is by no means common' (Palmer 1940). B Lloyd recorded it from Elstree and district in 1935, 1937 and 1939 and Palmer reported that it had been noted as occurring regularly at Hertford Heath.

By 1944, B Lloyd thought it was 'certainly widespread and by no means rare'. He noted that it will breed in small weedy ponds as well as large lakes (Lloyd 1944). In 1960 S Lloyd reported records from 1958 in areas as widely spread as Hertford Heath, Patmore Heath and Waterend (River Gade) (Lloyd 1960).

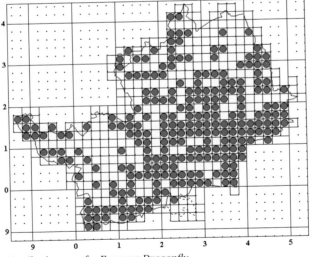

*Distribution map for Emperor Dragonfly*

During the 1960s reports were quite widespread, but it still did not seem to be reported very frequently and in 1974, not at all (Sage 1975).

The Emperor Dragonfly was recorded in 240 tetrads (52%) and is clearly both common and widespread. The few areas of the map where the distribution is fairly sparse coincide with areas of the county where there are few or no large areas of open water.

# Hairy Dragonfly
*Brachytron pratense* (Müller, 1764)

*Hairy Dragonfly*

The Hairy Dragonfly is the second least common dragonfly in Hertfordshire, after the White-legged Damselfly. It has an early flight season, usually emerging in the second week of May and finishing by the third week in June. During May it is usually the only hawker flying and therefore identification is straightforward. During June the Emperor Dragonfly is also on the wing, which complicates matters, although in reality they are quite different.

The Hairy Dragonfly is not a large hawker, being only 70% the size of an Emperor. The male has blue eyes, a hairy brown thorax with green antehumeral stripes. The abdomen is dark brown with two pear-shaped spots on each segment. The females have indistinct antehumeral stripes and yellow pear-shaped spots on the abdomen.

Male Hairy Dragonflies are usually seen patrolling reed-lined water bodies, hunting for insects and looking for females resting hidden in the vegetation. When a female is found, the male dashes into the vegetation to grasp the female and the pair fly off to commence copulation. As the males tend to keep close to the reed margins and frequently explore the bays in the emergent vegetation, they can be well camouflaged and difficult to see.

The first record of this dragonfly in Herts seems to have been by Stephens near Hertford in the 19th century (Lloyd 1949).

In the 20th century the first observation was also near Hertford, by Bertram Lloyd. His wife Sylvia described the occasion; 'Our first sight of this species in

Herts was in June 1939 by the New River near Hertford. My husband caught and identified a male here on 10th June. In bright light the males look blue-grey close at hand; the females duller, not bright coloured. This species does not show up much... it flies low, up and down over the surface along the edges of a canal or ditch, often very swiftly sometimes very slowly and hoveringly.

It has a habit of flying low in among thick reed or sedge or iris stems. Here at Hertford very thick sedges cover the whole ditch in parts; and the dragonfly was constantly flying through such patches low down – doubtless to pick insects off stems and leaves... sometimes they flew right into the reed beds.' From the description, it is possible that the site was Manifold Ditch.

After 1939, the Hairy Dragonfly was not seen again until 1950 when it was found on the Aylesbury Arm of the Grand Union Canal. It was seen there at fairly regular intervals, in small numbers, over the next decade. Several were also seen nearby at Wilstone Reservoir in 1952. Having last been recorded in 1962 at two places, one being at its former breeding ground on the Aylesbury Arm of the Grand Union Canal, it was not reported in Hertfordshire for 30 years. Then it was seen on 24th May 1992 at Cooks Wood near Harmer Green and, on 4th June 1995, at a pond at Datchworth (Gladwin 1996).

The Hairy Dragonfly, which was recorded in 31 tetrads (7%), is still a scarce species in Hertfordshire. Although there are a few records from the south, centre and northeast of the county, it is clear that the stronghold for this species is the Lea and Stort valleys.

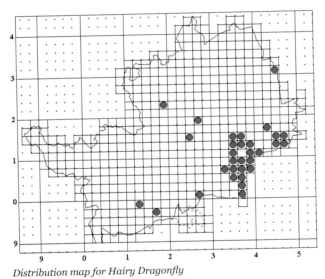

*Distribution map for Hairy Dragonfly*

# Four-spotted Chaser
*Libellula quadrimaculata* (Linnaeus 1758)

The Four-spotted Chaser, although not one of our most colourful dragonflies, always seems to be a favourite amongst dragonfly enthusiasts. The thorax and abdomen are both brown, with the abdomen merging to black over the last few segments. Like all chasers, the hind wings have black triangles at their base although, of course, the most significant feature is the four spots on the wings

*Four-spotted Chaser*

in addition to the four pterostigma. Both sexes are similar.

The only confusion species in Hertfordshire is the female Broad-bodied Chaser. However, the female Broad-bodied Chaser has a very broad abdomen, no black tail and has gold scallops at the side of the abdomen. It also resembles a Hornet in flight.

The Four-spotted Chaser is normally found flying around well-vegetated ponds, clashing frequently with other dragonflies. Fortunately, they settle quite often in characteristic pose with wings held forward, allowing good views and easing identification.

The flight season may start as early as the beginning of May and last until the third week of August, although the main season is from the third week of May until the third week of July.

Lucas (1900) describes it as having '...a liking for boggy pools... in general its flight is rapid, though of short duration'. It is a migratory species and a great wanderer. In 1930 Palmer reported, 'I do not know of any Herts locality where it breeds, and my only record is a single specimen taken at Digswell... 23th June 1921' (Palmer 1930). He quotes only one other record of which he was then aware, at Radlett, but with no details of date. By 1940 he only mentions one further sighting, 'a solitary specimen at Wain Wood near Hitchin, a long way from any water' (Palmer 1940).

In 1949 Sylvia Lloyd said this species is 'comparatively rare in Hertfordshire' (Lloyd, 1949). Later in the same volume she goes on to describe the first instance of breeding in the county, which she observed with her husband Bertram. 'On 27th June 1943, we spent some three hours at the small ponds, or rather old clay-pits by the Aylesbury Canal near Puttenham... there were five *L quadrimaculata* haunting the larger of the two ponds, with much growth of reed-mace in the water, where swaying on a blade, often near the tops thereof, they constantly perched after darting around at lightning speed... there were present... four males and one female'. They had watched the female ovipositing for some minutes in all parts of the pond.

During the 1950s and 1960s a few more records appear in the pages of the *Trans Herts NHS* from the Aylesbury Canal, Wilstone Reservoir, near Hoddesdon, at various sites in the Broxbourne Woods complex, etc. (Lloyd 1961; Sage 1964 and 1973). Egg laying was seen at a pond in Broxbourne Woods in June 1957. In 1959 Hodgson said it 'breeds regularly and is quite common on the Aylesbury Canal in the vicinity of Puttenham; also occurs, less frequently, at Wilstone Reservoir. One at Aldbury Nowers in 1952, one at Great Gaddesden in 1957' (Hodgson, 1959).

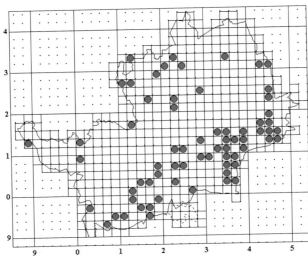

*Distribution map for Four-spotted Chaser*

The Four-spotted Chaser was clearly a scarce species in the 1900s and, as the distribution map shows, although it would appear to have increased and is widespread across the county, it is still not a common species.

It was recorded in only 67 tetrads (15%), which were concentrated in the south and east of the county.

## Broad-bodied Chaser
*Libellula depressa* (Linnaeus 1758)

The Broad-bodied Chaser is a very familiar species, being both distinctive and colourful and just as much at home around the garden pond as its usual haunts in shallow well-vegetated ponds in the countryside.

The males have a distinctive flattened, broad powder blue abdomen, which is edged with gold scallops. As for all chasers, there are conspicuous dark brown triangles at the base of the hind wings. Females are a beautiful golden brown, which becomes darker as they mature. When still freshly coloured they resemble hornets in flight.

For males the confusion species is the male Black-tailed Skimmer. However, the Black-tailed Skimmer has a slender abdomen, charcoal on the tail and no brown triangles at the base of the hind wings. For females the confusion species is the Four-spotted Chaser, but these have a slender abdomen, black tail and four spots on the wings in addition to the four pterostigma.

Like the Four-spotted Chaser, Broad-bodied Chasers spend most of their time dashing around ponds low over the water, hunting and looking for mates and continually clash with other dragonflies on the pond. Unlike the hawkers, chasers will frequently settle and tend to return to rest on a favourite perch, such as the top of a twig. This characteristic makes it easier for the observer to get a close look and identify the species securely. Their habit of settling on a convenient perch makes it possible to induce one to land on a stick pushed into the mud at the edge of a pond, if there is no naturally occurring perch.

The flight season may start as early as the beginning of May and last until the third week of August, although the main season is from the second week of May until the first week of August.

S Lloyd reported seeing one on 15th September (Lloyd 1948).

Palmer describes the Broad-bodied Chaser as, 'One of our commonest species, found in ponds

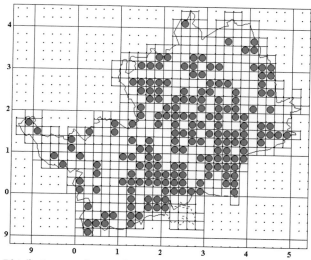

*Distribution map for Broad-Bodied Chaser*

and ditches all over the county... can occur in large numbers in spring' (Palmer 1930). B Lloyd said that, 'A dozen or more can often be watched in late May hunting low over the water around the margin of some quite small pond. Later they tend to spread over the countryside and are frequently seen far from water' (Lloyd 1944).

The Broad-bodied Chaser can be found all over the county, but appears to be less common in the western and northern areas. The species was recorded in 185 tetrads (40%).

## Black-tailed Skimmer
*Orthetrum cancellatum* (Linnaeus 1758)

*Black-tailed Skimmer*

Although Black-tailed Skimmers can on occasions be seen on wide open ditches, they are more normally associated with larger expanses of water, particularly those with beaches such as gravel pits and reservoirs. As their name suggests, they skim around low over the water at speed, periodically returning to the bank to settle, preferably on the mud or a stone.

Adult males have clear wings, a narrow powder blue abdomen and a charcoal coloured tip to the tail. Females and immature males also have clear wings, but the abdomen is straw coloured with a pair of 'L'-shaped markings on each segment.

The flight season may start as early as the third week of May and last until the middle of September, although the main season is from the fourth week of May until the third week of August.

Palmer did not mention this dragonfly in the 18 species he lists as recorded in Herts (Palmer 1930). B Lloyd believed he had the first Herts record, 'On 7 July 1935 I caught a male, after watching him for an hour on the wing and perching on a willow snag above the water... After identifying the insect I was of course careful to release it; but I did not see it or another of the species during several further visits in July'.

He went on to say, 'This appears to be the first record for Hertfordshire, into which county my insect flew from time to time while I watched him' (Lloyd 1937). His article is about dragonflies at Elstree (Aldenham) Reservoir and district so the sighting must be in that vicinity close to the county border (possibly the small section on the Fisheries Public House side of the road through which the county boundary runs). He saw the species again at Elstree (Aldenham) Reservoir in 1936 and 1937 (Lloyd 1938). However in 1939, he discovered an old record that showed it was previously recorded at Shenley in 1908 (Lloyd 1939).

Sylvia Lloyd (1949) described the field characters of the species. She calls it the 'Marsh Dragonfly' and goes on to say, 'The insect darts forward or dashes sideways for a stretch or swoops upwards with lightning rapidity... it is vastly partial to pitching on stony patches and expanding the wings to sun itself.' In the early 1950s she believed that this species was, 'none too common in the county' and 'considerably scarcer than some of its near relatives among the *Libellulidae* being generally seen singly, or at most in twos' (Lloyd 1952 & 1953).

By the 1960s and 1970s records become more common, especially at gravel pits and reservoirs, for example Rye Meads, Hilfield Park Reservoir and Park Street Gravel Pits (Sage 1966).

Whilst the Black-tailed Skimmer is well distributed across the county, it is not common in all areas. It was recorded in 120 tetrads (26.2%), which generally correlate with those areas of the county having large open areas of water.

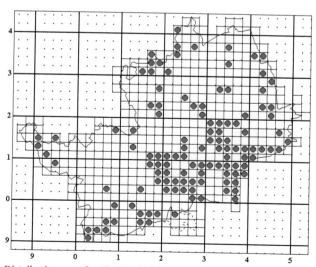

*Distribution map for Black-tailed Skimmer*

# Common Darter

*Sympetrum striolatum* (Charpentier 1840)

The Common Darter, in terms of flight season, is our longest flying dragonfly, being on the wing for nearly seven months. Although a few isolated individuals can be seen in early May, the full flush of emergence is not until the middle of June onwards. However, thereafter it can be seen on the wing until the first frosts which can be the end of November.

The males have red-brown eyes and an orangey-brown abdomen. When perched, the wings are held forward. Females have a straw-coloured abdomen. In both sexes the legs are brown, sometimes with an indistinct yellow line running down them.

The only confusion species are the Ruddy Darter, the migrant Yellow-winged Darter and the Large Red Damselfly. The Ruddy Darter is slightly smaller, has a 'pinched' or 'waisted' abdomen and, in both sexes, has jet-black legs. The males are crimson rather than the orangey-red of the Common Darter. Also, Common Darters have a small area of orange colouration at the base of the wings, which should not be confused with the Yellow-winged Darter, where the area of colouration is much larger (see Chapter 8). The Large Red Damselfly folds its wings along the abdomen when perched.

The Common Darter is very easy to observe at close quarters. Having selected a favourite perch at the edge of the water, which can be an area of dried mud, a stone, twig or a sprig of vegetation, it frequently launches into short bouts of darting flight, generally returning to the same perch.

Following emergence, the soft-skinned tenerals leave the water as soon as possible and seek refuge from predators by flying to neighbouring fields or

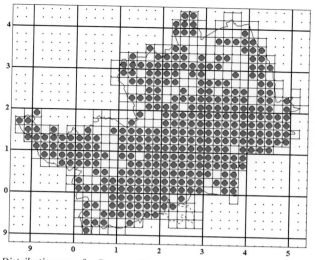

Distribution map for Common Darter

meadows. If you walk across these areas it is possible to disturb clouds of these insects, flying on their shiny new gossamer wings. They will stay away from water to dry out, hunt for food and mature and only then will they return to water to breed. Although, most other dragonfly species leave the vicinity of the water following emergence, it is particularly noticeable in the case of the Common Darter.

The Common Darter is included in Palmer's list of Hertfordshire dragonflies (Palmer 1930) and seems always to have been fairly common and widespread. Lucas (1900) says of its behaviour that it has 'very well developed the habit… of returning continually to the same spot, where it settles, often on the bare ground, after a short but exceedingly rapid flight'.

The Common Darter continues to be very common and widespread in the county. Being recorded in 345 tetrads (75.3%), the Common Darter is our most widespread dragonfly. The only areas where their occurrence is sparse are in the north and north west of the county where there are extensive areas of arable farmland.

## Ruddy Darter

*Sympetrum sanguineum* (Müller, 1764)

The Ruddy Darter must surely be one of the most striking dragonflies in Hertfordshire. The males have brown eyes and a vivid crimson abdomen, which is 'pinched' or 'waisted' about a third down from the thorax. The female has a straw-coloured abdomen. Both sexes have jet-black legs.

The only confusion species are the Common Darter, the migrant Yellow-winged Darter and the Large Red Damselfly. Male Common Darters have an orangey-brown abdomen. In both sexes the legs are brown and the abdomen is less 'pinched' or 'waisted'. Also, Ruddy Darters have a small area of orange colouration at the base of the wings, which should not be confused with the Yellow-winged Darter, where the area of colouration is much larger (see Chapter 8). The Large Red Damselfly folds its wings along the abdomen when perched.

Ruddy Darters can be found by any stretch of water, but are particularly fond of vegetation-lined ditches. Like the Common Darter, the Ruddy Darter is very easy to observe at close quarters. Having selected a favourite perch at the edge of the water, it frequently launches into short bouts of erratic flight, generally returning to the same perch.

The flight season may start as early as the beginning of June and last until the end of November, although the main season is from the middle of June until the first week of October.

Lucas (1900) said 'there are not many localities recorded for this species in Britain, but perhaps it only needs searching for and carefully discriminating from *S. striolatum*...' He described it as having, 'a short jerky flight, and often settles... it will often keep returning to the same spot'.

Sylvia Lloyd referred to this species both as the 'Scarce Crimson Dragonfly' (Lloyd 1948) and the 'Blood-red Dragonfly' (Lloyd 1949). She reported, 'This none too widely distributed species, of which a record for Hertfordshire exists as long ago as 1911, when Speyer noted 'a few' in the Shenley district, was not seen again until Bertram Lloyd recorded one male at Bricket Wood on 11th September 1938' (Lloyd 1948).

Bertram Lloyd described that sighting himself, 'On 11th September 1938 I watched and afterwards caught a single male near a pond at Bricket Wood. I saw no others thereabouts, either then or during two subsequent visits a little later in the month, though the weather was fine and sunny. It is therefore doubtful whether the insect which I caught, although it seemed very at home at the spot, had been bred in the vicinity' (Lloyd 1939).

In 1948 a specimen turned up at Elstree (Aldenham) Reservoir. Sylvia Lloyd was able to examine the insect closely and compare it with *S striolatum*. She noted that, 'the colour of the abdomen in *S sanguineum* is a much deeper richer crimson and also stouter, almost club shaped' (Lloyd 1948).

She reported on the species again in 1952. '*Sympetrum sanguineum*, which can still be regarded as extremely local in our county, was seen during a Field Meeting on 7th August 1948, at the Lily Pond, Wall Hall, Aldenham, and again near Otterspool in the same locality on 25th September of the same year.' By the following year she said it was, 'formerly very scarce', but now is, 'markedly on the increase' (Lloyd 1953).

During the 1950s and 1960s it is reported in the *Trans Herts NHS* at various sites including Bricket Wood, Hertford Heath, Shenley and Elstree (Aldenham) Reservoir, Northaw, Park Street, Tring Reservoirs, etc. but it never seems to be very common. As recently as 1992, Gladwin said that there was no confirmation that this species breeds in the county. However, in 1995 he was able to report that larvae had been found at Bricket Wood and Hertford Heath (Gladwin 1995).

Although the historical records suggest that the Ruddy Darter was once possibly scarce or even rare in the county, the distribution map shows that the species, although not common, is well distributed and established in the county.

As for many other species, the records are more common in the south, east and extreme west of the county where the habitat is more favourable.

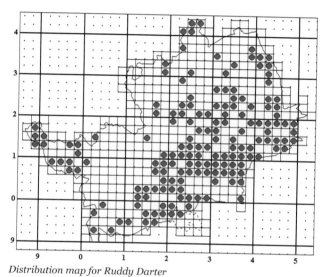

*Distribution map for Ruddy Darter*

# 6. Proof of breeding

During the Atlas Project, participants, in addition to recording the number of adult dragonflies or damselflies at a site, were encouraged to also record:

• The number of copulating pairs
• The number of ovipositing females
• The number of larvae present
• The number of exuvia present
• The number of freshly emerged tenerals

These data are useful, as they not only indicate that the species is present, but also provide an indication of whether the species is breeding.

On the 13th March 2004, the Dragonfly Conservation Group (DCG) under the umbrella of the British Dragonfly Society (BDS) established a set of criteria to assess the breeding status of a species. The criteria are as follows:

• **Successful Breeding**
  **Confirmed** – exuvia present (presence of an exuvia constitutes absolute proof that at least one specimen has completed a cycle from egg to adult at the site). Also emerging adults still in association with exuviae.
  **Probable** – larva present or female ovipositing or teneral (newly emerged adult) or regular presence of both sexes (normally annual presence in reasonable numbers or a repeated period consistent with the species' life-cycle length). All records to be at, or adjacent to, a suitable water body.

• **Possible Breeding** – pair copulating or female seen at a water body suitable for the species where at least one male has been observed to be engaged in some form of reproductive behaviour, such as territoriality or pursuing females.

The results of applying these criteria to the records collected during the Atlas Project show that, of the 19 species of dragonfly and damselfly regularly recorded in Hertfordshire, all satisfy the criteria for 'Successful Breeding Probable' and 'Possible Breeding', see the table below.

However, for the 'Successful Breeding Confirmed' category, only 14 species satisfied the criteria, the five species for which no exuvia were recorded being Red-eyed, Small Red-eyed and Emerald Damselflies, Hairy Dragonfly and Black-tailed Skimmer.

It is highly probable that these species do breed successfully in the county, but the necessary evidence in accordance with the BDS criteria is not available.

| Species | Successful Breeding Confirmed | Successful Breeding Probable | Possible Breeding |
|---|:---:|:---:|:---:|
| Banded Demoiselle | ✓ | ✓ | ✓ |
| Emerald Damselfly | ✗ | ✓ | ✓ |
| White-legged Damselfly | ✓ | ✓ | ✓ |
| Large Red Damselfly | ✓ | ✓ | ✓ |
| Red-eyed Damselfly | ✗ | ✓ | ✓ |
| Small Red-eyed Damselfly | ✗ | ✓ | ✓ |
| Azure Damselfly | ✓ | ✓ | ✓ |
| Common Blue Damselfly | ✓ | ✓ | ✓ |
| Blue-tailed Damselfly | ✓ | ✓ | ✓ |
| Migrant Hawker | ✓ | ✓ | ✓ |
| Southern Hawker | ✓ | ✓ | ✓ |
| Brown Hawker | ✓ | ✓ | ✓ |
| Emperor Dragonfly | ✓ | ✓ | ✓ |
| Hairy Dragonfly | ✗ | ✓ | ✓ |
| Four-spotted Chaser | ✓ | ✓ | ✓ |
| Broad-bodied Chaser | ✓ | ✓ | ✓ |
| Black-tailed Skimmer | ✗ | ✓ | ✓ |
| Common Darter | ✓ | ✓ | ✓ |
| Ruddy Darter | ✓ | ✓ | ✓ |

*Proof of breeding*

*Common Darter*

# 7. Flight periods

The collection of such a large quantity of dragonfly data over a six-year period provides a unique opportunity to produce a dragonfly flight chart specific to Hertfordshire. The table shows the flight periods of all the 19 regularly breeding species of dragonfly and damselfly that were recorded in Hertfordshire during the Atlas survey.

The main flight periods are shown in dark blue, and the build up and tail off periods are shown in light blue. There are noticeable variations in the emergence patterns of different species.

Dragonflies can be broadly classified as 'spring' or 'summer' species based on the degree of synchronisation of their emergence. Some 'spring' species such as the White-legged Damselfly, Azure Damselfly and Hairy Dragonfly have a well-synchronised emergence with only a short build up to the main flight period, and a well-defined end. For other 'spring' species such as the Large Red Damselfly, the emergence is well synchronised but then the flight season peters out over several weeks.

In four 'summer' species, the Banded Demoiselle, Emerald Damselfly, Southern Hawker and Common Darter, there is a more extended emergence period.

When planning visits to record certain species, it is strongly recommended that only the main flight period be used to ensure that the maximum numbers are flying.

*Right: Flight periods based on Hertfordshire Atlas data 2000-2005*

*Week 1 = 1st-7th      Week 2 = 8th-15th      Week 3 = 16th-23rd      Week 4 = 24th-31st*

*Key:* ■ *Main flight period* ■ *Build up and tail off*

| Month | Apr | | | May | | | | Jun | | | | Jul | | | | Aug | | | | Sep | | | | Oct | | | | Nov | | | |
|---|---|---|---|---|---|---|---|---|---|---|---|---|---|---|---|---|---|---|---|---|---|---|---|---|---|---|---|---|---|---|---|
| Week | 1 2 3 4 | 1 2 3 4 | 1 2 3 4 | 1 2 3 4 | 1 2 3 4 | 1 2 3 4 | 1 2 3 4 | 1 2 3 4 |
| Banded Demoiselle | | | | | | | | |
| Emerald Damselfly | | | | | | | | |
| White-legged Damselfly | | | | | | | | |
| Large Red Damselfly | | | | | | | | |
| Red-eyed Damselfly | | | | | | | | |
| Small Red-eyed Damselfly | | | | | | | | |
| Azure Damselfly | | | | | | | | |
| Common Blue Damselfly | | | | | | | | |
| Blue-tailed Damselfly | | | | | | | | |
| Migrant Hawker | | | | | | | | |
| Southern Hawker | | | | | | | | |
| Brown Hawker | | | | | | | | |
| Emperor Dragonfly | | | | | | | | |
| Hairy Dragonfly | | | | | | | | |
| Four-spotted Chaser | | | | | | | | |
| Broad-bodied Chaser | | | | | | | | |
| Black-tailed Skimmer | | | | | | | | |
| Common Darter | | | | | | | | |
| Ruddy Darter | | | | | | | | |

# 8. Rare migrants

The Atlas Project aimed to map the distribution of resident dragonfly and damselfly species across Hertfordshire based on data collected during the years 2000-05 inclusive. There are, however, a number of non-resident species that are recorded occasionally in the county which, although not strictly relevant to the Atlas Project, are still a part of the Hertfordshire dragonfly fauna. It is therefore appropriate to include a chapter on the status of these rare migrants based on records received both in and outside the Atlas study period.

The term 'migrant' denotes a species that would not normally be resident in the county, but has migrated from another area. Some species, for instance Yellow-winged Darter, are not resident in the UK and have migrated from the continent. In some years, these migrant dragonflies breed during their visit to the UK, although the colonies are not normally sustainable. Some other species, such as Black Darter and Keeled Skimmer, are found elsewhere in the UK and, for these species, it is not clear whether the insects are wanderers from UK colonies or are continental migrants.

Since 1999, a verification process has been in operation in Hertfordshire to assess the supporting evidence for each migrant record. For those records where it is considered that the written submission (often backed up with photographic evidence) is sufficient to confirm the sighting, the record is marked as verified on the database. In some instances it has been possible to verify records retrospectively. For some of the older records, it is not possible to apply the verification process and, accordingly, these records are marked on the database as not verified.

If a record is noted as not verified this does not imply that the identification was incorrect, but merely that there was insufficient supporting information for a verification process to be carried out.

Only those species that have been recorded since 1975 are included in this chapter. The historical records for the Beautiful Demoiselle, Scarce Emerald Damselfly, Scarce Blue-tailed Damselfly, Common Hawker and Downy Emerald are presented and discussed in Chapter 2.

The species addressed in the following sections are:

| | |
|---|---|
| Variable Damselfly | Yellow-winged Darter |
| Lesser Emperor | Black Darter |
| Keeled Skimmer | Vagrant Darter |
| Red-veined Darter | |

# Variable Damselfly

*Coenagrion pulchellum* (Vander Linden 1825)

*Variable Damselfly at Westbury Moat Ashwell 28th June 1996*

The Variable Damselfly has a distribution scattered over England, Scotland and Wales. However, the colonies, normally found in ditches and near slow-moving water, are often restricted to relatively small areas, which superficially appear to be no different from the surrounding habitat.

The male Variable Damselfly is very similar to the male Azure and Common Blue Damselflies, both of which can occur in similar habitats. The Variable Damselfly does, however, appear slightly thinner and darker due to the higher percentage of black markings, and the antehumeral stripes are normally broken, often resembling exclamation marks. Finally, on segment two, the U shape is normally joined to the black band below giving the appearance of a wine glass or goblet.

The Variable Damselfly is not normally found in Hertfordshire and the nearest known colonies are in Cambridgeshire.

There have been four records of Variable Damselfly in Hertfordshire. Two of the records are from the 1920s and have not been through the verification process. The third record was of a colony found at a pond in Watery Grove, Stevenage, where one of the insects was caught and the identification confirmed. Unfortunately the species could not be refound following extensive management of the pond in 1971. The fourth record from Westbury Moat at Ashwell was verified by photograph (shown above).

The list of Hertfordshire records for Variable Damselfly is given below:

| Date | Site | Grid | No | Verified |
|------|------|------|-----|----------|
| 1924 | Woodhall Park, Watton-at-Stone | - | A | ✗ |
| 1929 | Home Park, Hatfield | - | A | ✗ |
| 1969 | Watery Grove, Stevenage | - | Col | ✓ |
| 28/06/96 | Westbury Moat, Ashwell | TL262394 | A | ✓ |

A = 1   B = 2-5   C = 6-20   + = present   Col = colony
✓ = verified   ✗ = insufficient evidence for verification

## Lesser Emperor
*Anax parthenope* (Sélys 1839)

*Lesser Emperor*

The Lesser Emperor is widespread across Europe with increasing numbers being recorded in the UK each year.

It is a medium-sized hawker which is slightly smaller than the Emperor. It has green eyes, a green-brown thorax and an olive abdomen. The key distinguishing feature is the blue-violet ring at the base of the abdomen on segments two and three. In flight, it also holds its abdomen out straight compared to the droopy abdomen of the Emperor. At a distance, both sexes are similar.

The Lesser Emperor regularly breeds in the UK at a few sites with an increasing number of sightings, some of which have probably been bred locally.

There have been three reports of Lesser Emperor in Hertfordshire. The first was of a pair at Hilfield Park Reservoir on the 2nd July 2006. The second and third records were on the 26th and 27th July 2006 at Wilstone Reservoir and were probably the same insect. All these records have been verified.

The list of Hertfordshire records for Lesser Emperor is given below:

*Lesser Emperor records in Hertfordshire*

| Date | Site | Grid | No | Verified |
|---|---|---|---|---|
| 02/07/06 | Hilfield Park Reservoir | TQ1494 | B | ✓ |
| 26/07/06 | Wilstone Reservoir | SP902132 | A | ✓ |
| 27/07/06 | Wilstone Reservoir | SP902132 | A | ✓ |

A = 1   B = 2-5   C = 6-20   + = present
✓ = verified   ✗ = insufficient evidence for verification

# Keeled Skimmer

*Orthetrum coerulescens* (Fabricius 1798)

*Keeled Skimmer at Bury Green, Bishops Stortford 10th July 2003*

The Keeled Skimmer is usually associated with streams, ditches and pools within areas of acid bog.

The male has clear wings and a narrow pale blue abdomen. Females are straw coloured. The main confusion species are the Black-tailed Skimmer, which can be distinguished by a black tip to the abdomen and both Scarce and Broad-bodied Chasers, which have black triangles at the base of the hind wings.

There have been four records in Hertfordshire. The first three are regarded as uncertain although there is no doubt about the fourth, which was verified by photograph.

The list of Hertfordshire records for Keeled Skimmer is given below:

*Keeled Skimmer records in Hertfordshire*

| Date | Site | Grid | No | Verified |
|------|------|------|-----|----------|
| Pre 1911 | Shenley | - | A | ✕ |
| 1945 | Hatfield Great Wood | - | A | ✕ |
| 30/08/52 | Wilstone Reservoir | - | A | ✕ |
| 10/07/03 | Bury Green, Bishops Stortford | TL448213 | A | ✓ |

A = 1    B = 2-5    C = 6-20    + = present
✓ = verified    ✕ = insufficient evidence for verification

# Red-veined Darter
*Sympetrum fonscolombii* (Sélys 1840)

*Red-veined Darter at Wilstone Reservoir 25th June 2006*

The Red-veined Darter is predominantly a Mediterranean species extending from Greece to Spain, although spasmodic migrations can take the species north to Belgium, Holland, northern Germany, Poland and the UK (Askew 1988). It is now being increasingly recorded in the UK with widespread yet local breeding colonies appearing.

Male Red-veined Darters may be readily distinguished from our resident Common and Ruddy Darters by the scarlet abdomen and the red venation in the half of each wing adjacent to the abdomen. In females, the abdomen and venation is yellow.

The 15 Hertfordshire records for Red-veined Darter, listed below, reflect the now increasingly frequent migratory behaviour of this species.

*Red-veined Darter records in Hertfordshire*

| Date | Site | Grid | No | Verified |
|------|------|------|----|----------|
| 1908 | Shenley | - | B | ✗ |
| 1908 | Aldenham Reservoir | - | A | ✗ |
| 22/05/92 | Hilfield Park Reservoir | TQ161961 | A | ✓ |
| 09/06/96 | Hollycross Lake, Amwell Quarry | TL378131 | A | ✓ |
| 20/06/98 | Broxbourne Gravel Pits | TL378072 | A | ✓ |
| 21/06/98 | Tyttenhanger Gravel Pits | TL192059 | B | ✓ |
| 18/06/00 | Tyttenhanger Gravel Pits | TL193050 | A | ✓ |
| 01/07/01 | Folly Farm, Bulbourne | SP944142 | B | ✓ |
| 30/06/02 | Tyttenhanger Gravel Pits | TL195051 | B | ✓ |
| 14/07/02 | Tyttenhanger Gravel Pits | TL195051 | A | ✓ |
| 16/06/06 | Wilstone Reservoir | SP902132 | A | ✓ |
| 17/06/06 | Hilfield Park Reservoir | TQ154963 | A | ✓ |
| 17/06/06 | Wilstone Reservoir, Drayton Beauchamp | SP903127 | C | ✓ |
| 17/06/06 | Wilstone Reservoir | SP902132 | C | ✓ |
| 25/06/06 | Wilstone Reservoir | SP902132 | B | ✓ |

A = 1   B = 2-5   C = 6-20   + = present

✓ = verified   ✗ = insufficient evidence for verification

# Yellow-winged Darter

*Sympetrum flaveolum* (Linnaeus 1758)

*Yellow-winged Darter at Hertford Heath 19th August 2006*

The Yellow-winged Darter is common in southern, central and eastern Europe, and is very abundant in Siberia and Japan (Askew 1988). It is an infrequent visitor to the UK, but there have been a few migration years when it has arrived in large numbers. However, despite breeding attempts during these years, it has not succeeded in colonising.

The male Yellow-winged Darter is very similar to our more common Ruddy Darter, but is easily distinguished by the amber patches at the base of the wings. The Ruddy Darter can display small amber patches at the base of the wings, but on the Yellow-winged Darter the amber area covers a third of each of the fore wing and hind wing. The females have similar colouration on the abdomen as female Ruddy Darters.

In Hertfordshire there have been 37 records, 34 of which occurred in 1995, which was the last major eruption. During this year Yellow-winged Darters were observed at 17 different sites in August, and ovipositing observed at Amwell Quarry (now Amwell Nature Reserve), Hertford Heath, Panshanger and Wilstone Reservoir, Tring. The largest numbers counted were 25 at Hertford Heath on 20th, 13 at Amwell Quarry on 12th, and 10 at Wilstone Reservoir from 5th to 21st, and Hilfield Park Reservoir and Panshanger on 12th August. The other three records were at Bricket Wood Common in 1926, at Smallford Lake near St Albans on 4th September 1996 and at The Roundings, Hertford Heath on 19th August 2006.

The list of Hertfordshire records for Yellow-winged Darter is given below:

| Yellow-winged Darter records in Hertfordshire | Date | Site | Grid | No | Verified |
|---|---|---|---|---|---|
| | 1926 | Bricket Wood Common | TL130010 | A | ✗ |
| | 18/09/69 | River Mimram, Tewinbury | TL264139 | A | ✓ |
| | 1995 | River Oughton, Oughtenhead | TL166304 | + | ✓ |
| | 1995 | Hertford Heath, Goldingtons | TL354110 | + | ✓ |
| | 1995 | Frogmore Hall Pit, Aston | TL285205 | C | ✓ |
| | 1995 | Wilstone Reservoir | SP902132 | + | ✓ |
| | 1995 | River Colne and Colney Heath Common | TL203058 | + | ✓ |
| | 1995 | Wilstone Reservoir | SP905128 | C | ✓ |
| | 03/08/95 | Silvermeade, Lee Valley Park | TL372063 | A | ✓ |
| | 03/08/95 | Tringford Reservoir, Tring | SP918132 | A | ✓ |
| | 03/08/95 | Hertford Heath, Roundings | TL349106 | C | ✓ |
| | 04/08/95 | Hertford Heath, Roundings | TL349106 | B | ✓ |
| | 05/08/95 | Hertford Heath, Roundings | TL349105 | B | ✓ |
| | 05/08/95 | Rye House Marsh | TL385105 | A | ✓ |
| | 06/08/95 | Cheshunt Pits, Lee Valley Park | TL375030 | B | ✓ |
| | 06/08/95 | River Stort, Sawbridgeworth | TL488150 | A | ✓ |
| | 11/08/95 | Rye Meads | TL387100 | A | ✓ |
| | 11/08/95 | Hertford Heath, Roundings | TL349106 | A | ✓ |
| | 12/08/95 | Hertford Heath, Roundings | TL349106 | B | ✓ |
| | 12/08/95 | Amwell Quarry | TL377130 | C | ✓ |
| | 12/08/95 | River Gade, Charlotte's Vale | TQ086987 | A | ✓ |
| | 12/08/95 | Digswell Recreation Ground | TL246148 | B | ✓ |
| | 12/08/95 | Panshanger Park | TL292128 | C | ✓ |
| | 13/08/95 | River Colne and Colney Heath Common | TL201059 | B | ✓ |
| | 13/08/95 | Tyttenhanger Gravel Pits | TL190050 | C | ✓ |
| | 16/08/95 | Silvermeade, Lee Valley Park | TL372063 | A | ✓ |
| | 19/08/95 | Stockers Lake, Rickmansworth | TQ052936 | B | ✓ |
| | 19/08/95 | Hertford Heath, Roundings | TL349106 | C | ✓ |
| | 20/08/95 | Hertford Heath, Roundings | TL349105 | D | ✓ |
| | 22/08/95 | Hilfield Park Reservoir | TQ158960 | B | ✓ |
| | 25/08/95 | Amwell Quarry | TL377130 | A | ✓ |
| | 26/08/95 | Amwell Quarry | TL378131 | A | ✓ |
| | 26/08/95 | Hertford Heath, Roundings | TL 350105 | B | ✓ |
| | 03/09/95 | Hertford Heath, Roundings | TL349106 | A | ✓ |
| | 18/09/95 | Hilfield Park Reservoir | TQ155959 | A | ✓ |
| | 04/09/96 | Smallford Lake, St Albans | TL197071 | A | ✓ |
| | 19/08/06 | Hertford Heath, Roundings | TL349105 | A | ✓ |

A = 1   B = 2-5   C = 6-20   + = present

✓ = verified   ✗ = insufficient evidence for verification

# Black Darter

*Sympetrum danae* (Sulzer 1776)

*Black Darter at Hertford Heath 28th July 2002*

The Black Darter is an attractive small insect generally associated with acidic bogs in heathland and moorland. It is not a breeding species in Hertfordshire, nor is it regularly recorded, but does appear from time to time as a migrant. The Black Darter is known to be a wanderer.

Male Black Darters are very conspicuous with their black colouration and yellow markings and are therefore readily distinguishable from the other darters. The main confusion occurs late in the season when mature female Common Darters can become a blue-grey colour and are on occasion mistaken for Black Darters. Because of this potential confusion, Black Darter records are scrutinised meticulously as are all records of migrant species. The females are similar in appearance to female Ruddy Darters, but can be distinguished by the black triangle on top of the thorax.

There have been 13 records of Black Darter in Hertfordshire and the 12 records since 1956 have all been verified. All but one of these records have come from Patmore Heath or Hertford Heath, which are both HMWT reserves having a small amount of suitable habitat. Unfortunately, the ponds at both sites are prone to drying out during hot weather and are therefore unable to sustain a breeding population.

The list of Hertfordshire records for Black Darter is given below:

| Date | Site | Grid | No | Verified |
|---|---|---|---|---|
| 1929 | Digswell | - | A | ✗ |
| 06/10/56 | Patmore Heath NR | TL443257 | C | ✓ |
| 1960 | Patmore Heath NR | TL443257 | + | ✓ |
| 05/08/73 | Patmore Heath NR | TL443257 | B | ✓ |
| 1975 | Patmore Heath NR | TL443257 | + | ✓ |
| 11/09/75 | Ardeley | TL3026 | A | ✓ |
| 11/09/75 | Patmore Heath NR | TL443257 | B | ✓ |
| 25/09/87 | Patmore Heath NR | TL443257 | + | ✓ |
| 15/07/91 | Patmore Heath NR | TL443257 | A | ✓ |
| 03/09/95 | Hertford Heath NR, Goldingtons, Crab Tree Pond | TL354111 | A | ✓ |
| 28/07/02 | Hertford Heath NR, Brick Ponds | TL349106 | A | ✓ |
| 31/07/02 | Hertford Heath NR, Brick Ponds | TL349106 | A | ✓ |
| 04/08/02 | Hertford Heath NR, Brick Ponds | TL349106 | A | ✓ |

A = 1   B = 2-5   C = 6-20   + = present

✓ = verified   ✗ = insufficient evidence for verification

## Vagrant Darter

*Sympetrum vulgatum* (Linnaeus 1758)

The Vagrant Darter, although common in central and northeast Europe, is an extremely rare, yet maybe overlooked, migrant to the UK that is sometimes associated with influxes of Yellow-winged Darters.

The Vagrant Darter is very similar to the Common Darter but has clear wings with no hint of yellow at the base of the wings. Also, the black stripe at the top of the frons extends down the side of the frons, a feature that can clearly be seen when the specimen is examined in the hand. The extension of the black stripe down the side of the frons is also present on the Ruddy and Red-veined Darters.

The males are redder than male Common Darters with a slightly pinched abdomen. Females have yellow-brown abdomens like female Common Darters, but the vulvar scale is at right angles to the abdomen and is less prominent than on other darter species. Both sexes have dark legs with a yellow stripe.

The year 1995 was particularly memorable for the large numbers of migrant darters reaching Britain. Two Vagrant Darters, the first authenticated records for the county, were observed during this period. Tom and Janet Gladwin caught and photographed a male at Panshanger on 12th August, and Stephen

Smith provided a detailed description of one he observed at Tyttenhanger the following day.

The two Hertfordshire records for Vagrant Darter are given below:

*Vagrant Darter records in Hertfordshire*

| Date | Site | Grid | No | Verified |
|------|------|------|-----|----------|
| 12/08/95 | Panshanger Park | - | A | ✓ |
| 13/08/95 | Tyttenhanger | - | A | ✓ |

A = 1   B = 2-5   C = 6-20   + = present

✓ = verified   ✗ = insufficient evidence for verification

# 9. Species richness and evaluation of sites

## Introduction

As stated previously, a total of 14,671 records were collected during the six years of the Atlas Project. This large number of records not only allows distribution maps to be produced, but also permits other analyses to be performed such as:

a. Which species has the highest number of records?
b. Which species occurred in the highest abundance?
c. Which species was recorded in the most tetrads?
d. Which sites supported the most species?

The results of the analyses are given in the following sections.

## The most recorded species

This section looks at the number of records collected for each species and provides a list, which ranks the species in order of how common they are in the county. In this section it is the *frequency* of occurrence, not the recorded *abundance* for each species that is being investigated. The results are shown below.

*Blue-tailed Damselfly, the most frequently recorded species in Hertfordshire*

| Species | No of records | % |
|---|---|---|
| 1.  Blue-tailed Damselfly | 1802 | 12.3 |
| 2.  Azure Damselfly | 1780 | 12.1 |
| 3.  Common Darter | 1515 | 10.3 |
| 4.  Common Blue Damselfly | 1292 | 8.8 |
| 5.  Large Red Damselfly | 990 | 6.7 |
| 6.  Southern Hawker | 969 | 6.6 |
| 7.  Brown Hawker | 953 | 6.5 |
| 8.  Banded Demoiselle | 917 | 6.3 |
| 9.  Emperor Dragonfly | 837 | 5.7 |
| 10.  Migrant Hawker | 792 | 5.4 |
| 11.  Broad-bodied Chaser | 662 | 4.5 |
| 12.  Ruddy Darter | 633 | 4.3 |
| 13.  Black-tailed Skimmer | 473 | 3.2 |
| 14.  Red-eyed Damselfly | 403 | 2.7 |
| 15.  Emerald Damselfly | 218 | 1.5 |
| 16.  Four-spotted Chaser | 214 | 1.5 |
| 17.  Hairy Dragonfly | 120 | 0.8 |
| 18.  (Small Red-eyed Damselfly) | 49 | 0.3 |
| 19.  White-legged Damselfly | 44 | 0.3 |
| 20.  (Red-veined Darter) | 5 | - |
| 21.  (Black Darter) | 3 | - |

There are some surprises. It would probably have been expected that the most frequently recorded species in Hertfordshire would be the Azure Damselfly. In fact it was narrowly nudged into second place by the Blue-tailed Damselfly with 1802 records (12.3%). The Common Darter was third, pushing the Common Blue Damselfly into fourth position.

The Small Red-eyed Damselfly, Red-veined Darter and Black Darter are all shown in brackets in this section and subsequent ranking, as their results are not significant. The Small Red-eyed Damselfly appeared in the county for the first time during the Atlas Project and is therefore not properly represented, and the two darters are both rare migrants whose appearance in Hertfordshire is sporadic.

## The species recorded in the highest numbers

This section investigates which species were recorded in the highest numbers on a single visit.

During the Atlas Project, the numbers of each species seen were recorded using an alphabetical code as follows:

A = 1
B = 2-6
C = 7-20
D = 21-100
E = 101-500
F = 500+

Therefore, to determine which species had been recorded in the highest numbers, the Atlas records were analysed to find out which species had been recorded under the three top categories ie F, E or D. The results in descending order are given in the table below.

*The species recorded in the highest numbers*

| No of records in each category | F (500 +) | E (101-500) | D (21-100) |
|---|---|---|---|
| 1. Common Blue Damselfly | 24 | 78 | 201 |
| 2. Common Darter | 2 | 1 | 44 |
| 3. Blue-tailed Damselfly | 1 | 7 | 106 |
| 4. Banded Demoiselle | - | 36 | 93 |
| 5. Azure Damselfly | - | 30 | 232 |
| 6. Red-eyed Damselfly | - | 7 | 54 |
| 7. Large Red Damselfly | - | 1 | 29 |
| 8. Black-tailed Skimmer | - | 1 | 28 |
| 9. Ruddy Darter | - | 1 | 23 |
| 10. White-legged Damselfly | - | 1 | 5 |
| 11. Emerald Damselfly | - | - | 16 |
| 12. Migrant Hawker | - | - | 14 |
| 13. Brown Hawker | - | - | 3 |
| 14. Small Red-eyed Damselfly | - | - | 3 |
| 15. Broad-bodied Chaser | - | - | 2 |
| 16. Emperor Dragonfly | - | - | 1 |
| 17. Hairy Dragonfly | - | - | 1 |
| 18. Southern Hawker | - | - | 1 |

The table shows that the species recorded in by far the largest numbers was the Common Blue Damselfly, with an amazing 25 records showing that over 500 damselflies were seen in a single visit and 78 records showing that between 101 and 500 were observed. To anyone who has witnessed Common Blue Damselflies swarming over a large lake on a hot summer's day, this may have been expected.

What may be unexpected is that second place does not go to another damselfly, but the Common Darter, with two records of single visit sightings where over 500 insects were reported.

However, surely the biggest surprise of all is the record of over 500 Blue-tailed Damselflies at Admirals Walk Lake, Hoddesdon. Blue-tailed Damselflies are both common and widespread, but do not normally occur in such large numbers.

Fourth and fifth places go to the Banded Demoiselle and Azure Damselfly, both with over 30 records of between 101 and 500 insects noted.

One interesting feature is that the White-legged Damselfly had one record between 101 and 500 damselflies and five others of between 21 and 100. This illustrates the point that, although the White-legged Damselfly is the least widespread of the resident Hertfordshire dragonflies if we count the number of tetrads in which it has been recorded, it is locally abundant along the Aylesbury Arm of the Grand Union Canal at Wilstone. In fact, just over the border in Bedfordshire and Buckinghamshire, this species is common.

Not surprisingly the hawkers, being more solitary, end the list, with only the Migrant Hawker having a significant number of records in Category D. The only species not recorded in categories D-F was the Four-spotted Chaser.

## The species recorded in the most tetrads

This section identifies the species that have been recorded in the most tetrads and are therefore the most widely distributed species. The results (excluding the rare migrants) are shown in the table below.

*The species recorded in the most tetrads*

| Species | No of tetrads | % |
|---|---|---|
| 1. Common Darter | 345 | 75.3 |
| 2. Blue-tailed Damselfly | 326 | 71.2 |
| 3. Azure Damselfly | 319 | 69.7 |
| 4. Common Blue Damselfly | 267 | 58.3 |
| 5. Emperor Dragonfly | 240 | 52.4 |
| 6. Southern Hawker | 240 | 52.4 |
| 7. Brown Hawker | 238 | 52.0 |
| 8. Migrant Hawker | 235 | 51.3 |
| 9. Large Red Damselfly | 188 | 41.0 |
| 10. Broad-bodied Chaser | 185 | 40.4 |
| 11. Banded Demoiselle | 171 | 37.3 |
| 12. Ruddy Darter | 161 | 35.2 |
| 13. Black-tailed Skimmer | 120 | 26.2 |
| 14. Red-eyed Damselfly | 97 | 21.2 |
| 15. Emerald Damselfly | 67 | 14.6 |
| 16. Four-spotted Chaser | 67 | 14.6 |
| 17. Hairy Dragonfly | 31 | 6.8 |
| 18. (Small Red-eyed Damselfly) | 19 | 4.1 |
| 19. White-legged Damselfly | 14 | 3.1 |

The top three in the ranking are the Common Darter, Blue-tailed Damselfly and the Azure Damselfly, all being recorded in over 70% of the 458 tetrads.

Eight species were recorded in more than 50% of the tetrads and ten of the 19 Hertfordshire species were recorded in 40% or more of the tetrads.

## The best sites

The distribution maps show that most dragonfly species are fairly common and are well distributed across the county. However, it is inevitable that there will be some sites that are particularly attractive to dragonflies and will support a large number of species. So where are they?

The records were analysed to find out which sites had the most regular Hertfordshire species recorded and the top 26 sites with 14 or more species recorded during the six-year duration of the Atlas Project are listed below.

| | Site | No of species | Place |
|---|---|---|---|
| *Sites with 14 or more species* | Amwell Nature Reserve | 19 | 1st |
| | King's Meads Nature Reserve | 18 | 2nd |
| | Admirals Walk Lake | 17 | = 3rd |
| | Hilfield Park Reservoir** | 17 | = 3rd |
| | Silvermeade | 17 | = 3rd |
| | Berrygrove Wood | 16 | = 6th |
| | Fir and Pond Woods Nature Reserve | 16 | = 6th |
| | Frogmore and Moor Mill GPs | 16 | = 6th |
| | Grand Union Canal, Aylesbury Arm | 16 | = 6th |
| | Henry Moore Foundation Pond | 16 | = 6th |
| | Hertford Heath Nature Reserve | 16 | = 6th |
| | Brent Pelham* | 15 | = 12th |
| | Broxbourne GPs* | 15 | = 12th |
| | Cheshunt Park | 15 | = 12th |
| | Smallford Lake* | 15 | = 12th |
| | Swanland Road Lagoons | 15 | = 12th |
| | Woodhall Park* | 15 | = 12th |
| | Bedwell Park Golf Club* | 14 | = 18th |
| | Bowyers Water | 14 | = 18th |
| | Broad Colney | 14 | = 18th |
| | Butterwick Field* | 14 | = 18th |
| *\* Private site* | Hollingson Mead | 14 | = 18th |
| *\*\* Restricted* | Mill Green GC* | 14 | = 18th |
| *access – HMWT* | Stanstead Abbotts GP | 14 | = 18th |
| *members can* | Turnford and Cheshunt GPs | 14 | = 18th |
| *obtain key* | Waterford Heath | 14 | = 18th |

The top site for the county is Amwell Nature Reserve where all 19 resident species were recorded. Hollycross Lake at Amwell has a very diverse habitat combining shallow margins, deep water with floating vegetation, trees and well-vegetated banks. It is also one of the few sites in Hertfordshire to record White-legged Damselfly.

The second best site is King's Meads with 18 species; King's Meads also has a very diverse habitat with large lakes, ponds and a system of ditches, but not really any habitat suitable for White-legged Damselfly.

*King's Meads Nature Reserve*

There were three sites with 17 species, Admirals Walk Lake, Hilfield Park Reservoir and Silvermeade.

It is worth noting that of the 11 sites having 16 or more species, five are HMWT Trust reserves. However, please note that Hilfield Park Reservoir has restricted access. Trust members can collect a key to the reserve from the HMWT headquarters at Grebe House in St Albans.

Please also note that the list includes a number of private sites. For these sites it was only possible to collect data for the Atlas Project with the kind permission of the landowners. The sites are included for completeness, but their inclusion should not be interpreted as granting access.

The top ten sites, with unrestricted public access and 16 or more species recorded are described in more detail in the chapter on 'Where To Watch Dragonflies and Damselflies in Hertfordshire'.

# 10. Where to watch dragonflies in Hertfordshire

## Introduction

Analysis of the records collected during the Atlas Project provided a valuable insight into the distribution and populations of dragonflies in Hertfordshire. The ranking section not only identified the most widespread and numerous species, but also highlighted the sites in the county where the highest number of dragonfly species were seen.

The top ten sites having unrestricted public access, in alphabetical order, are as follows:

1. Admiral's Walk Lake
2. Amwell Nature Reserve
3. Berrygrove Wood
4. Fir and Pond Woods Nature Reserve
5. Grand Union Canal Aylesbury Arm
6. Henry Moore Foundation Pond
7. Hertford Heath Nature Reserve
8. King's Meads Nature Reserve
9. Moor Mill and Frogmore Gravel Pits
10. Silvermeade Nature Reserve

A map showing the location of the sites is given below.

*The best sites in Hertfordshire*

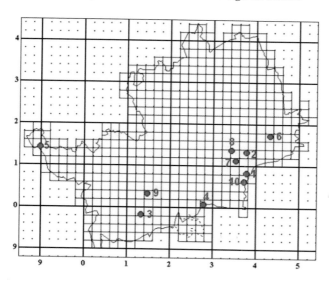

Most of the best sites are concentrated in the south and east of the county. The only exception is the Aylesbury Arm of the Grand Union Canal.

The following sections provide information that will hopefully encourage both seasoned Odonatists and beginners to visit these sites, which collectively exhibit a wide variation in dragonfly habitats and between them support all 19 of the resident county species.

The information on each site covers:

a. A map of how to get there
b. A larger scale map of the site where applicable
c. Parking
d. Access points
e. Description of the site
f. Key areas and key species

Many of the sites are spread across a wide area and in these instances the map reference given is the centre of the site.

The key to the maps is as follows:

↑        NORTH UP THE PAGE

———      SITE BOUNDARY

———      RIVER OR STREAM

———      RAILWAY

═══      ROAD

- - - -  FOOTPATH

●        ACCESS POINT

●        RAILWAY STATION

P        PARKING

NB: Please note that the maps are not to scale.

We hope that you will find the information useful and enjoy your visits.

# Admirals Walk Lake

Situated: East of Hoddesdon
Map Reference: TL377082
Managed by: Lee Valley Regional Park Authority
Conservation Status: Nil
Dragonflies: 17 species

Admirals Walk Lake is a 10 hectare (25 acre) fishing lake to the east of Hoddesdon. The lake is flanked by a private horse paddock to the west and a railway to the east.

Enter the Lampits housing estate from Charlton Way and park along the straight section of road opposite house numbers 116–122 (TL376085). Walk down the footpath opposite house number 118 and, after 100m, turn right across the footbridge over the New River. Turn left along the river footpath for 20 m and then enter the horse paddock via the metal kissing gate. The paddock is private but there is a public footpath along the northern boundary so therefore keep to the fence on the left.

Once through the paddock, continue on to the kissing gate on your right just before the bridge over the River Lynch. Go through the gate and there is a footpath that takes you along the north and west sides of the lake.

The nearest railway station is Broxbourne, 700m to the south. However, there is no direct link between the station and the lake and the route via Broxbourne High Street is more likely to be 2.5km.

The lake has an open aspect with only a minimal numbers of trees along the banks. There is no floating or emergent vegetation and the marginal vegetation is predominantly rush and Reed Canary Grass.

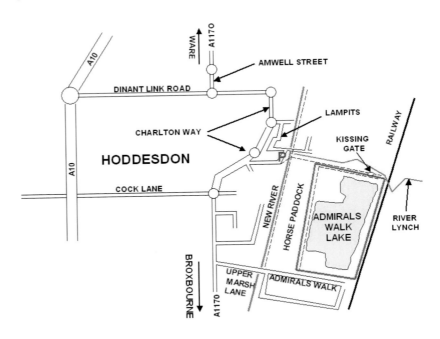

The lake supports 17 species of dragonfly including the White-legged Damselfly and the Hairy Dragonfly. The only resident Hertfordshire species missing are the Small Red-eyed and Emerald Damselflies. As the Red-eyed Damselfly is present, there is a strong possibility that the Small Red-eyed Damselfly will colonise the site in due course.

## Amwell Nature Reserve

Situated: South of Ware
Map Reference: TL376132
Managed by: Herts and Middlesex Wildlife Trust
Conservation Status: Ramsar Site, Special Protection Area (SPA) and Site of Special Scientific Interest (SSSI)
Dragonflies: 19 species

Amwell Nature Reserve in the Lea Valley south of Ware, is a complex of former gravel pits excavated between 1973 and 1990. The initial excavations were carried out by St Albans Sand and Gravel, which then became RMC Aggregates, who were later taken over by Cemex. Cemex continued ownership until December 2006 when it was bought by HMWT.

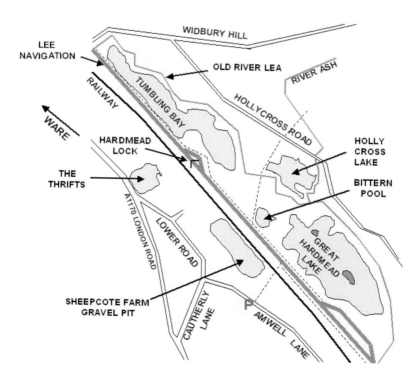

The nature reserve includes Great Hardmead Lake, the Bittern Pool, Hollycross Lake and the southern end of Tumbling Bay. There is no waterside access to Great Hardmead Lake or the Bittern Pool. However, a dragonfly trail to Hollycross Lake, which is the key dragonfly site and supports all 19 of the county species, is open to visitors during the summer months.

Park in Amwell Lane at TL374125. Walk up the track signposted Footpath 17 and Amwell Nature Reserve, over the railway and the Lee Navigation and turn left along the Lee Navigation towpath. Walk past the James hide and Bittern Pool on your right and at the footbridge over the Lee Navigation turn right up the track that takes you up the hill.

Cross the footbridge over the Old River Lea and continue to walk along the path through the trees. The entrance to Hollycross Lake is on your right, just before you get to Hollycross Road. Go through the kissing gate to the lake. Please note that grazing cattle are present and that NO DOGS ARE ALLOWED AROUND HOLLYCROSS LAKE.

Hollycross Lake offers a diverse habitat including large expanses of water with extensive patches of lily pads, sheltered bays with both emergent and submerged vegetation and a well-vegetated ditch.

The nearest railway station is St Margaret's, which is 1.3km southeast of the Bittern Pool. As you leave the station, turn left and left again onto the Lee Navigation towpath, which will bring you to Amwell Nature Reserve.

# Berrygrove Wood

Situated: Aldenham
Map Reference: TQ133981
Managed by: Hertfordshire County Council
Conservation Status: Nil
Dragonflies: 16 species

Berrygrove Wood is owned and managed by Hertfordshire County Council. This mixed woodland is part of the 405ha (1000 acre) Wall Hall Estate that was bought in 1947 to preserve the green belt. Once managed for its sporting interest, Berrygrove is now a working woodland, showing how commercial timber harvesting can be successfully combined with both conservation and recreation.

Park outside the Aldenham Golf and Country Club (TQ138983), or alternatively park by the church and walk back. Take the footpath that runs along the edge of the field next to Dairy Cottages. Once inside the wood, follow one of the footpaths shown on the map to the pond.

The nearest railway station is Watford North, a distance of 3.5km by road from Aldenham Golf and Country Club.

Although the pond is deep inside a wood, it has a reasonably open aspect with plenty of open water. The vegetation is almost exclusively marginal and emergent rush, but there is also some submerged vegetation.

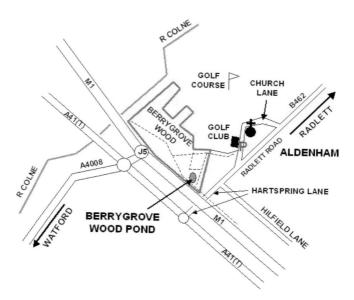

The pond supports 16 species of dragonfly, the only resident Hertfordshire species absent are the Red-eyed, Small Red-eyed and White-legged Damselflies, which is not surprising as the habitat is not suitable for these species.

# Fir and Pond Woods Nature Reserve

Situated: Southeast of Potters Bar
Map Reference: TL278005
Managed by: Herts and Middlesex Wildlife Trust for Herts County Council
Conservation Status: County Wildlife Site
Dragonflies: 16 species

This oak-hornbeam woodland is a remnant of the Enfield Chase, an ancient royal hunting forest that once covered 8,000ha (19,760 acres). Its great value lies in its diversity of habitat, which supports an abundance of wildlife.

Park in the lay-by opposite the entrance to the Oshwal Centre in Coopers Lane Road (TL277012). Go through the wooden kissing gate and follow the track down the edge of Fir Wood. At the end of Fir Wood, go through two wooden kissing gates and enter Pond Wood. Take the track to your left and follow the footpath along the edge of the wood.

The path takes you along the northern boundary of the wood and then along the eastern boundary and eventually brings you to Turkey Brook. Cross the bridge over the brook and there is an observation platform that overlooks the largest of the ponds.

Old pond is 120m x 100m and has an open aspect. However, there is a broad

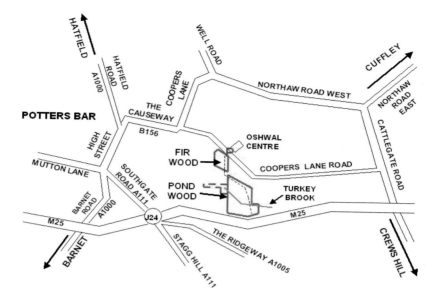

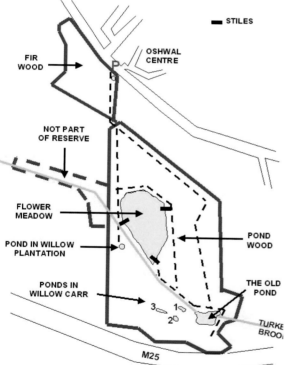

band of Bulrush around its margin, up to 30m wide in places, which makes viewing difficult. The best sites for watching dragonflies are the three smaller ponds to the west of the large pond.

These three ponds are well hidden in the willow carr. Walk westwards along the southern bank of Turkey Brook and the first pond can be seen through the trees. This pond, Pond 1, is 30m x 15m and has an open aspect with marginal and emergent Reed Sweet Grass and Bulrush, marginal Gipsywort and large expanses of floating Broad-leaved Pondweed.

Pond 2 is further south going towards the motorway and is accessed from the southern corner of Pond 1. This pond is 20m x 15m and also has an open aspect but is fringed with willow on all sides. Otherwise, the vegetation is similar to Pond 1.

Pond 3 is further west and is also accessed from the southern corner of Pond 1. This pond is 30m x 10m and is fringed with willows on all sides with marginal and emergent Reed Sweet Grass, marginal Gipsywort and some floating Broad-leaved Pondweed. At the western end there is a substantial stand of Bulrush.

There is also a 10m diameter circular pond in the willow plantation west of the flower meadow. This pond is set in the middle of a large stand of Bulrush with marginal and emergent rush and Floating Sweet Grass, marginal Gipsywort, emergent Water Cress and Branched Bur-reed.

Another pond by the entrance to Fir Wood is very shaded and covered with duckweed, but often attracts Southern Hawkers.

The ponds collectively support 16 species of dragonfly, the missing species being White-legged, Red-eyed and Small Red-eyed Damselflies. The habitat is suitable for the latter two species, but perhaps difficult for the insects to find in a woodland setting.

The nearest railway station is Potters Bar, a distance of 3.5km by road.

## Grand Union Canal Aylesbury Arm

Situated: West of Wilstone
Map Reference: SP896142
Managed by: British Waterways
Conservation Status: Nil
Dragonflies: 16 species

The Aylesbury Arm of the Grand Union Canal west of Wilstone not only supports a large number of species of dragonfly but also is undoubtedly the

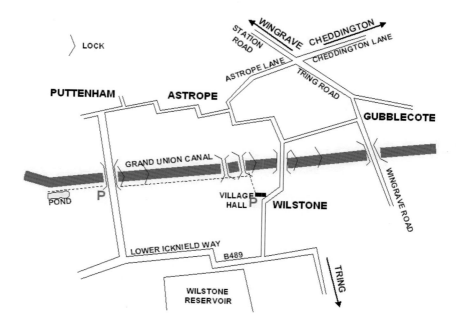

best place in Hertfordshire to see the White-legged Damselfly. This species is the least widespread dragonfly in Hertfordshire although is quite common in Buckinghamshire, which probably accounts for their presence at this site. Although they are relatively common here, they are much less common and apparently declining at other similar habitats in the county, such as the Lea Valley. It is not entirely clear why this is the case.

Park in the Wilstone Village Hall car park at SP903142. Walk across the football pitch behind the hall, keeping to the left. Continue through the picnic area and onto the Grand Union Canal Aylesbury Arm towpath. Turn left and walk past Gudgeon Stream No 9 Lock and the footbridge.

Once past the footbridge, the near side bank becomes well vegetated and it is from here to the next lock that the White-legged Damselfly can be seen. If you visit the site at the height of the flight season, usually June and July, they should not be difficult to find, as along this stretch of the canal, they are by far the commonest species of dragonfly.

There is also a pond worth visiting at SP885139. It can be reached by continuing to walk along the towpath, under the next road bridge, and the pond is 450m on your left. Alternatively, you can park next to the road bridge at SP889140. There is sufficient off-road parking for 4-5 cars.

The Grand Union Canal and pond support 16 species of dragonfly, the missing species being the Small Red-eyed Damselfly, Hairy Dragonfly and Black-tailed Skimmer. It is not really surprising that the latter two species are absent as the habitat is not suitable. However, if it continues to spread as rapidly as it has done so far, the Small Red-eyed Damselfly may colonise the site in the not too distant future.

# Henry Moore Foundation Pond

Situated: South of Much Hadham
Map Reference: TL433170
Managed by: Part of Henry Moore Foundation Estate
Conservation Status: Nil
Dragonflies: 16 species

The Henry Moore Foundation at Perry Green was established in 1977 to promote fine arts, in particular the work of Henry Moore. The pond is situated at the southwest corner of the estate, and is 'guarded' by a 6.75m high bronze sculpture at the eastern end. Although the pond is on the private estate, there is a footpath running past it.

Park at the corner of the road (TL434170), being careful not to obstruct the gate or the field entrance. Also, be warned that there is only space for 2-3 cars. Go through the gate and the pond is on your left.

The pond is 100m long x 30m wide and contains both marginal and emergent rush, with emergent Bulrush at one end and down the centre. Unfortunately, the banks are heavily grazed and therefore there is no marginal vegetation except that at the waters edge.

The pond supports 16 species of dragonfly including the scarce Hairy Dragonfly. The missing species are the White-legged and Small Red-eyed Damselflies and the Black-tailed Skimmer. The absence of the White-legged Damselfly and the Black-tailed Skimmer is to be expected, as the habitat is not suitable. However, as Red-eyed Damselflies are present, then it may only be a

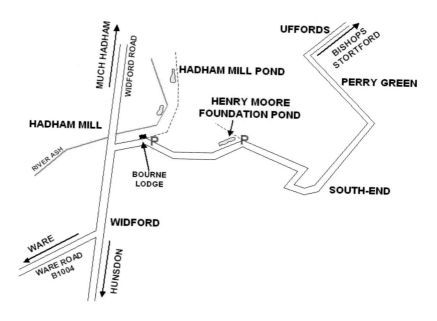

matter of time before Small Red-eyed Damselflies become established.

Another nearby site that is worth a visit is Hadham Mill Pond. Park off the road at the entrance to the wood by Bourne Lodge (TL425169). Follow the footpath, passing a pond on your left on the other side of the River Ash. Hadham Mill Pond is further on to the left of the footpath, a total distance of 1km.

The pond is mainly tree-lined but has plenty of emergent sedge, and supports ten species of dragonfly including the Red-eyed Damselfly.

## Hertford Heath Nature Reserve

Situated: Hertford Heath, 1.5 miles southeast of Hertford
Map Reference: TL354111
Managed by: Herts and Middlesex Wildlife Trust for Haileybury
Conservation Status: Site of Special Scientific Interest (SSSI)
Dragonflies: 16 species

Hertford Heath Nature Reserve covers 25ha (62 acres) and is in two sections located on either side of the B1197, which runs through the village of Hertford Heath. For both sections park in Roundings at the side of The College Arms (TL352109). The nearest railway station is Hertford East, a distance of 3.5km.

The section to the north of the B1197, Goldingtons, is a woodland area consisting of mature hornbeam coppice and secondary oak and birch. From

The College Arms, cross the B1197 and go up Heath Lane and enter the wood. Take the track on the right, which will bring you to Crabtree Pond. A number of dragonfly species can be seen here, in particular Large Red Damselfly, which are very numerous early in the season, Ruddy Darters, Emerald Damselflies and being a woodland pond, there are frequent sightings of Southern Hawker. Also, look out for Purple Hairstreak butterflies around the oak trees that line the pond.

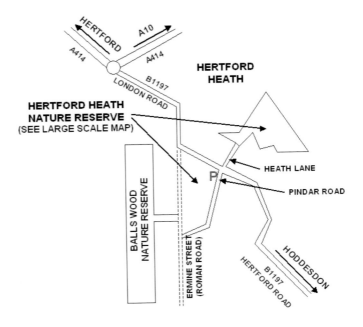

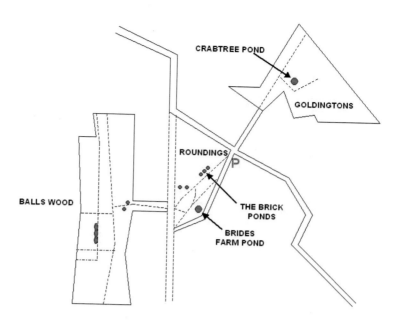

The section to the south of the B1197, the Roundings, is an area of damp heathland and there are a number of pools with sphagnum mosses and rushes. From The College Arms go down Pindar Road leading to Roundings Road and enter the reserve via the first track by the reserve sign. Follow the path through the wood and onto the heath by the wooden bench.

The ponds in front of you are the 'brick ponds' which are the result of excavating clay from what was once open grazed heathland. These ponds tend to dry up when rainfall is low for prolonged periods, but when they hold water are rich in dragonfly fauna. The clay was used to make bricks on site, to construct the small row of cottages in Roundings Road, next to The College Arms. The cottages, built in ca.1805, were for the staff of the new East India College, which subsequently became Haileybury College, the owners of the site.

There are also two further ponds southwest of the brick ponds, close to Ermine Street, the Roman road.

Between them these ponds support 16 species of dragonfly, the only missing species being Red-eyed, Small Red-eyed and White-legged Damselflies, which is not surprising as the habitat is not suitable for these species. Also, over the years, there have been records of both Black and Yellow-winged Darters (see the chapter on rare migrants).

There is another larger pond opposite Brides Farm (TL350105). This pond is more wooded than the ponds on the heath and therefore frequently attracts Southern Hawkers.

Whilst in the area, it would be worth visiting the ponds in Balls Wood, another HMWT Nature Reserve.

From Brides Farm pond, continue down Roundings Road to the intersection with Ermine Street. Turn right and, after 100m, the entrance is on your left.

The northern part of the wood is the oldest and varies from old hornbeam coppice, which is now very mature, to mixed woodland of Ash and Field Maple. Aspen has become more abundant in recent years. Throughout the wood there are a number of grassy rides.

There are two ponds either side of the main ride, which are both worth a visit. Also, further into the wood, along one of the lateral rides there are a series of interlinking ponds, which usually attract a variety of dragonflies.

The open sunny rides attract good numbers of White Admiral butterflies during the summer months and later in the season swarms of Migrant Hawkers can be seen patrolling up and down looking for prey.

## King's Meads Nature Reserve

Situated: Between Hertford and Ware
Map Reference: TL344138
Managed by: Herts and Middlesex Wildlife Trust for various owners
Conservation Status: County Wildlife Site
Dragonflies: 18 species

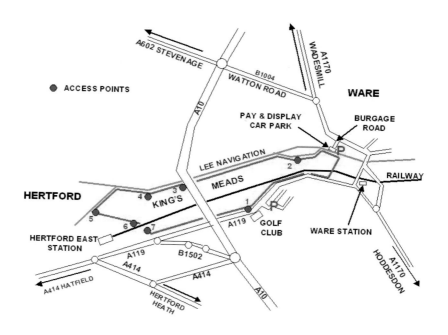

King's Meads, between Hertford and Ware, is a complex of the largest remaining grazed riverside flood meadows in Hertfordshire, covering 96ha or 237 acres. The rivers and ditches, which criss-cross the site, traditionally flooded the flat land although, due to falling water levels, this now happens less often than in the past. However, ditch restoration and the maintenance of a system of sluices is gradually restoring the water levels to the meadows during the winter months. This combination of ditches, floodwater and regular grazing has created a rich wetland habitat that is excellent for a range of flora and fauna.

These water meadows consist of a number of meads including Park Mead, Stockade Mead, Hollow Mead, King's Mead, Sweet Mead, Lady's Mead, Widow's Mead, Mill Mead, Little Mead, Tansy Mead and Broad Mead, collectively known as King's Meads. King's Mead itself lies centrally on the site under the A10 flyover and to the north of the New River. Collectively known as King's Meads Nature Reserve, the site is managed by HMWT on behalf of the owners and partners, namely East Herts Council, Environment Agency, GlaxoSmithKline, Thames Water Utilities and a private landowner.

There are two areas for parking. The first is the residential area immediately east of Chadwell Spring Golf Club on the A119 (TL352137). Alternatively, at weekends, it is possible to park in front of the business units immediately west of the golf club (TL348136). From here, entry to the site is via Access Point 1 shown on the map.

The second parking area is a Pay and Display car park next to the library at Burgage Road, which is a turning off Ware High Street (TL357143). Leave the car park via the footbridge over the Lee Navigation, turn right and follow

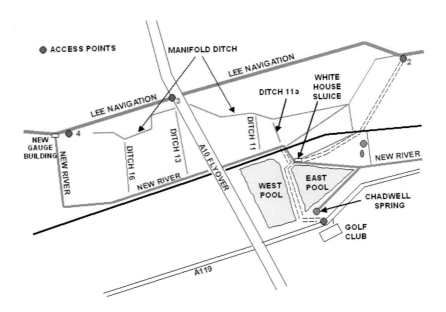

the towpath towards the flyover. Entry to the site can then be made via Access Point 2 at Ware Lock or Access Point 3 under the flyover.

The site can also be reached by rail from either Hertford East or Ware station. From Hertford East, follow Mead Lane (north of the railway track) and enter the site at Access Point 6. From Ware station follow the New River footpath west, which will bring you to White House Sluice shown on the large-scale map above.

King's Meads have a wide variety of dragonfly habitats. West Pool is a large area of floodwater, which is host to large colonies of Common Blue Damselfly and Black-tailed Skimmer. It can, however, dry out during periods of drought. The stream that runs northeast towards the railway from White House Sluice is a reliable place to see Banded Demoiselles, as well as Migrant Hawkers later in the season. The New River supports a large colony of Common Blue Damselflies and, despite having little floating vegetation, also attracts a few Red-eyed Damselflies.

The other key sites are Ditches 11, 11a, 13, 16 and Manifold Ditch west of the flyover. All of the 18 species of dragonfly can be seen on these ditches, with spectacular views of the scarce Hairy Dragonfly from mid May until mid June. The only missing species is the White-legged Damselfly due to the lack of suitable habitat.

Please note that grazing cattle are present.

# Moor Mill and Frogmore Gravel Pits

Situated: Park Street, St Albans
Map Reference: TL147032
Managed by: -
Conservation Status: Part of Moor Mill is an SSSI for geological reasons
Dragonflies: 16 species

Frogmore Pits once provided good quality gravel for road building. The lakes and surrounding area, including Moor Mill to the south, are landscaped former gravel workings and can now be used for fishing and walking. Frogmore Gravel Pits is also the site of an ancient settlement, dating back thousands of years.

Park in the car park at the end of Hyde Lane (TL151032) and walk across the footbridge over the River Ver where there should be good numbers of Banded Demoiselle.

A little further on there are four lakes, numbered 1-4 on the large scale map. The ponds are all different in character including tree-lined banks, stands of water lilies and gravelly beaches, which accounts for the large number of species present. Three of the four lakes support the Red-eyed Damselfly.

The Frogmore Gravel Pits support 15 of the 16 species present on the

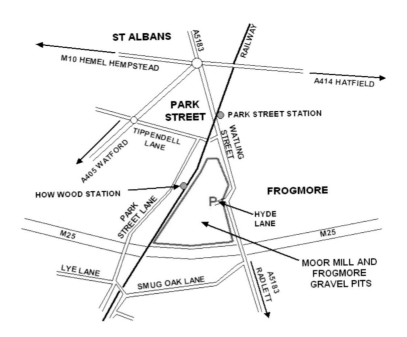

site, the missing species being the Emerald Damselfly. For this species it is necessary to visit the seasonal ponds on the large expanse of grassland on Moor Mill.

Walk westward along the path between Lakes 2 and 4 towards How Wood Station. At the end of the path just before you get to the railway, there is a kissing gate on your left. This leads you on to Moor Mill.

Here there are a number of seasonal ponds, all having an open aspect with plenty of marginal and emergent rush and Bulrush.

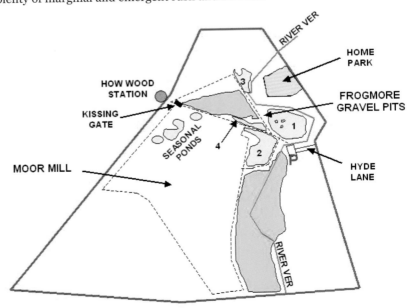

The sites support 16 species of dragonfly, the missing species being the White-legged and Small Red-eyed Damselflies and the Hairy Dragonfly. However, as the Red-eyed Damselfly is present, there is a strong possibility that the Small Red-eyed Damselfly will colonise the site in due course.

## Silvermeade Nature Reserve

Situated: East of Broxbourne
Map Reference: TL372063
Managed by: Lee Valley Regional Park Authority
Conservation Status: County Wildlife Site
Dragonflies: 17 species

Silvermeade Nature Reserve is situated to the southeast of Broxbourne and is part of the Lee Valley Park. It is nine hectares (22 acres) of grazed water meadow with a number of drainage ditches.

There are two parking areas. For the first, go down Mill Lane from the A1170 and continue to the end (TL372068). Here there are two car parks. Once parked, leave the car park by the way you came in and turn right along the footpath, which takes you under the railway. Turn right and walk into the Boat Car Park (TL373068).

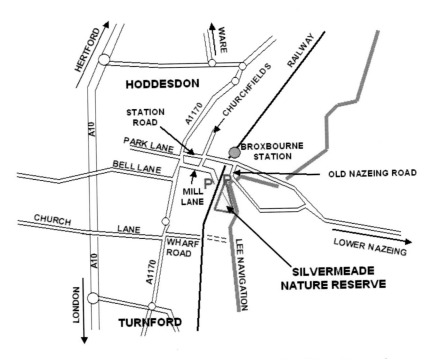

The second option is to park in the boat car park itself, but this may be busy during the summer months, particularly at weekends. The boat car park is accessed by going down Station Road and turning right into Old Nazeing Road. The boat car park is at the bottom of the hill on your right. Broxbourne railway station is 500m to the north of the boat car park, the other side of Station Road.

From the car park, turn right into Old Nazeing Road and after 30m turn right again onto the Lee Navigation towpath (signposted Old Mill and Meadows and Silvermeade). After 30m go over the footbridge and turn right into Silvermeade via the kissing gate. Continue into Silvermeade for 250m, keeping close to the railway, until you reach the main ditch.

This ditch runs diagonally across the site from the railway in the north to the Lee Navigation in the south, where it joins up with another ditch that runs down the eastern boundary.

The main ditch has both emergent and marginal sedge and reed and supports 17 species including the rare White-legged Damselfly and the scarce Hairy Dragonfly. The missing species are the Small Red-eyed and Emerald Damselflies. As the Red-eyed Damselfly is present, there is a strong possibility that the Small Red-eyed Damselfly will colonise the site in due course.

Please note that grazing cattle may be present.

## Appendix A: Glossary of terms

### Dragonflies or damselflies?

One of the most commonly asked questions is 'When you talk about dragonflies, does that include damselflies?'

And the answer is 'It depends'.

The confusion arises from the family tree, which is shown below.

*Family tree*

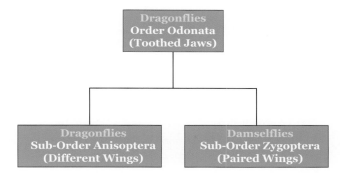

Dragonflies are in the insect Order *Odonata*, which means 'toothed jaws'. *Odonata* includes two sub-orders, *Anisoptera* (dragonflies) and *Zygoptera* (damselflies) and hence the confusion. Throughout this book the term dragonfly shall mean both dragonflies and damselflies.

*Anisoptera* means 'different wings' referring to the fact that dragonfly forewings are a different shape to the hindwings. *Zygoptera* means 'paired wings' as the forewings and hindwings of damselflies are the same shape (see Anatomy below).

### Anatomy

The basic anatomy of a damselfly is shown below.

Damselflies are delicate insects with a fluttering flight. They are usually gregarious and on warm sunny days some species, such as the Common Blue Damselfly, can be seen over open water in swarms of up to a 1000. At rest, damselflies generally fold their wings over the top of the abdomen.

Damselflies have a rectangular-shaped head, with large eyes on either side. On the outer leading edge of the forewing there is a dark cell called the

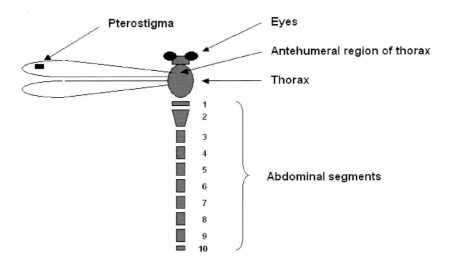

Pterostigma

Eyes

Antehumeral region of thorax

Thorax

1
2
3
4
5
6
7
8
9
10

Abdominal segments

*Basic anatomy
of a damselfly*

pterostigma, which some believe acts as a counterbalance during flight. In some species the colouration of the pterostigma can aid identification.

Damselfly bodies have three main body parts: head, thorax and abdomen. Behind the head is the thorax, which supports the wings. For damselflies, the forewings and the hindwings are the same shape.

Behind the thorax is the abdomen, which is divided into ten segments. Segments one and ten are very narrow and sometimes difficult to see. Segment two is the most conspicuous being the transitional segment between the wide thorax and the narrow abdomen. However, from an identification point of view, it is the markings on segments two, three, eight and nine that are the most important as they are key to the identification of most of the blue damselflies.

The anatomy of an *Anisopteran* dragonfly is similar to that of a damselfly, except that the head is spherical and is almost entirely covered by a pair of large eyes. Also, the forewings and hindwings are of a different shape.

Anisopteran dragonflies are robust and strong fliers and are seldom seen in the high numbers often associated with damselflies. Also when at rest, unlike damselflies, they hold their wings at right angles to their abdomen and some species, such as the chasers and darters, hold their wings pointing forward in an almost threatening posture.

# Definitions

**Abdomen**  The hind part of the body attached to the thorax

**Abdominal segment**  One of ten segments of the abdomen

**Antehumeral stripes**  Stripes along the antehumeral region of the thorax

**Frons**  The front mask of the face

**Ovipositing**  Egg-laying

**Pterostigma**  A dark cell on the outer leading edge of the forewing, which some believe acts as a counterbalance during flight

**Thorax**  That part of the body between the head and the abdomen, which supports the wings and legs

**Teneral**  A freshly emerged adult dragonfly

**Venation**  The system of veins running through the wings

**Vulvar scale**  A flap below segment eight in females

# Appendix B: Gazeteer

All sites where dragonflies were recorded are listed.

| | | | |
|---|---|---|---|
| Aberford Park, new lake, Borehamwood | TQ189977 | Astonbury Wood Lake | TL277215 |
| Aberford Park, old lake, Borehamwood | TQ192973 | Astonbury Wood north | TL275213 |
| Admirals Walk Lake N, Hoddesdon GP | TL377082 | Astonbury Wood Pasture Pond | TL277215 |
| Admirals Walk Lake S, Hoddesdon GP | TL376078 | Astonbury Wood ponds  Bragbury End | TL275213 |
| Albury End pond | TL430236 | Astonbury Wood, Daphne's pond | TL275216 |
| Albury estate, low gravel pond | TL434253 | Astonbury Woods Crocodile pond | TL273215 |
| Albury Hall Conduit pond | TL426254 | Astrope, Millhoppers pasture/adj meadows | SP899149 |
| Albury Hall Kitcher's Pond | TL430257 | Austage End | TL162254 |
| Albury pond in field nr church | TL438248 | Ayot Green Village pond | TL220139 |
| Albury, ditch E of Water Tower | TL425245 | Ayot Green West pond | TL218140 |
| Albury, Oaken Spring, pond | TL434259 | Ayot Greenway Black Bridge | TL194146 |
| Aldbury | SP963123 | Ayot Greenway Sparrow Hall Bridge | TL205143 |
| Aldbury Nowers | SP950130 | Ayot Place | TL212150 |
| Aldbury Nowers, Duchies Piece | SP952129 | Ayot Place Warren Wood | TL207148 |
| Aldbury Stock's Farm | SP963131 | Ayot St Lawrence | TL191172 |
| Aldenham Church | TQ141985 | | |
| Aldenham Country Park | TQ165963 | Baas Hill pond | TL358071 |
| Aldenham GC pond at edge | TQ136986 | Bakers End farmland | TL395170 |
| Aldenham Reservoir, East | TQ171955 | Bakers End pond | TL395170 |
| Aldenham Reservoir, West | TQ166957 | Baldock Services | TL234365 |
| Allens Green Blounts Farm | TL458179 | Baldock, London Road | TL247333 |
| Allens Green pond | TL455169 | Balls Park | TL337120 |
| Alnwick Farm Pond 1 | SP891176 | Balls Park lagoon Hertford | TL337118 |
| Alnwick Farm Pond 6 in field | SP892177 | Balls Wood NR and ponds | TL344105 |
| Alnwick Farm ponds | SP892177 | Banfield Wood | TL322222 |
| Alnwick Farm Ponds 2, 3, 4 | SP892177 | Barkway | TL385357 |
| Alswick Hall ornamental pond | TL377294 | Barkway east of Earls Wood | TL401355 |
| Amwell Quarry (N) Hollycross Lake | TL376133 | Barkway The Grove Earls Wood pond | TL397350 |
| Amwell Quarry (SE) Hardmead Lake | TL381124 | Barkway, Brickhill Grove pond | TL399357 |
| Amwell Quarry (SW) Hardmead Lake | TL376129 | Barkway, Church Lane pond | TL382355 |
| Amwell Quarry ditch | TL377133 | Barkway, Earls Wood pond | TL393352 |
| Anstey pond nr Church | TL404329 | Barkway, School pond | TL383355 |
| Aquadrome, Rickmansworth | TQ055940 | Barley Broadmoor Pond | TL397395 |
| Ardeley Village pond | TL308272 | Barnes Wood ponds | TL256168 |
| Ashridge Estate, Ashridge Golf Club pond | SP989123 | Bassus Green | TL303257 |
| Ashridge Estate, Prince's Riding | SP983126 | Bassus Green Lords Wood | TL316255 |
| Ashridge Estate, Thunderdell Wood pond | SP982126 | Bassus Green St Johns Wood pond | TL310255 |
| Ashridge Forest, Aldbury Common, pond | SP974125 | Batchworth Heath pond | TQ077924 |
| Ashwell End | TL258408 | Batchworth Lake | TQ056942 |
| Ashwell North | TL270406 | Batford Springs LNR | TL146150 |
| Ashwell North Mobbs Hole Ditch | TL263438 | Bayford | TL311085 |
| Ashwell Village | TL263399 | Bayford Lake | TL315097 |
| Ashwell West End Garden pond | TL263392 | Bayford Manor House lake | TL313084 |
| Ashwell, Northfield | TL260420 | Bayfordbury Lake  Hertford | TL313102 |
| Aspenden ditch | TL349284 | Bayfordbury Park Farm | TL314111 |
| Aspenden pond, site one | TL348288 | Bedmond Birch Wood, Bedmond Lane | TL123054 |
| Aspenden ponds site two | TL354283 | Bedmond Ninnings Field | TL101037 |
| Aston End Frogmore | TL270240 | Bedmond Twitchell's Farm | TL100043 |
| Aston End, Tatlers Lane | TL271239 | Bedwell Pk GC Bridge Pond | TL282088 |
| Aston Golf Course pond | TL269221 | Bedwell Pk GC E Central | TL284086 |
| Aston, Sacombe Corner Wood SW | TL284216 | Bedwell Pk GC Fallen oak pond | TL280078 |

| | |
|---|---|
| Bedwell Pk GC Far Pond | TL280097 |
| Bedwell Pk GC Narrow marshy pond | TL279074 |
| Bedwell Pk GC NE | TL280090 |
| Bedwell Pk GC North end pond | TL279098 |
| Bedwell Pk GC NW | TL278091 |
| Bedwell Pk GC Ornamental Lake | TL280085 |
| Bedwell Pk GC Pond SE of Big clubhouse | TL279075 |
| Bedwell Pk GC Reedy pond | TL280077 |
| Bedwell Pk GC Sandpit Grove Big Pond | TL281079 |
| Bedwell Pk GC Sandpit Grove Small Pond | TL280079 |
| Bedwell Pk GC Twin Pond N | TL282086 |
| Bedwell Pk GC Twin Pond S | TL282085 |
| Bedwell Pk GC W Central | TL270080 |
| Bedwell Pk GC Woodside Pond | TL282083 |
| Beech Farm GP North | TL194087 |
| Beech Farm GP South | TL196087 |
| Beech Farm GP West | TL189089 |
| Beech Hyde Farm | TL184129 |
| Beechwood Home farm Cheveralls Green | TL037154 |
| Bell Bar, Bell Lane pond | TL253053 |
| Bencroft Wood  Horseshoe pond | TL329064 |
| Bengeo Temple Farm | TL339179 |
| Beningon Lordship farm pond in field | TL293238 |
| Benington crossroads pond | TL298237 |
| Benington Lordship ponds | TL297236 |
| Bennington Lordship Farm pond | TL293238 |
| Bentley Heath Church pond | TQ249996 |
| Bentley Heath ponds | TQ250996 |
| Bentley Heath village pond | TQ249996 |
| Berkesdon Green Spring, pond | TL328278 |
| Berkhamsted Ashlyn's Farm | SP986067 |
| Berkhamsted Common | SP989113 |
| Berkhamsted GC Pond by 10th tee | TL005089 |
| Berkhamsted GC Pond nr War memorial | TL005095 |
| Berkhamsted Marlin Chapel Farm | SP963073 |
| Berrygrove Wood | TQ128985 |
| Berrygrove Wood pond  Aldenham | TQ133981 |
| Biggins Farm east of Barwick Ford | TL397191 |
| Biggins Farm North | TL398196 |
| Binghams plantation, Aldenham | TQ128990 |
| Birch Green garden pond | TL290118 |
| Birch Green ponds | TL292118 |
| Birch Green village pond | TL291118 |
| Birchwood JMI pond Hatfield | TL225094 |
| Birklands Field Pond, St Albans | TL168050 |
| Bishops Stortford, West Road | TL484207 |
| Blackhorse Farm | TL242347 |
| Blackthorn Wood pond | TL266117 |
| Blagrove Common, stream | TL328337 |
| Blounts Farm | TL458179 |
| Boarscroft Farm ditch to east | SP881167 |
| Borehamwood, garden pond | TQ204966 |
| Bourne End Church | TL016065 |
| Bourne End footpath | TL015035 |
| Bovingdon Brick pit 3 | TL006028 |
| Boxted Farm Pond nr Hemel Hempstead | TL030086 |
| Bramfield House Lake | TL294156 |
| Bramfield Wood  Bramfield | TL288166 |
| Bramfield Woods ponds | TL283171 |
| Bramfield, Bramfield Park Wood | TL285155 |
| Braughing Green End, Bingles Wood, Pond | TL389248 |

| | |
|---|---|
| Breachwood Green Hillside Farm garden pond | TL156222 |
| Breachwood Green The Pheasantry garden pond | TL149224 |
| Breachwood Green The Spinney garden pond | TL149225 |
| Brent Pelham Beeches Wood | TL444314 |
| Brent Pelham Hall | TL436308 |
| Brent Pelham woodland ponds | TL444308 |
| Brickendon GC Pembridge Lane pond | TL323076 |
| Brickendon Grange GC, Clubhouse Pond | TL317077 |
| Brickendon Grange Golf Club Pond | TL315074 |
| Brickendon village pond  nr.Hertford | TL323079 |
| Bricket Wood Black Green | TL132025 |
| Bricket Wood Common(SE) Pound pond, School Lane | TL132008 |
| Bricket Wood Common, Brimstone Glade pond | TL132006 |
| Bricket Wood Common, pond in woods | TL129008 |
| Bricket Wood East, Watermeadows & pools N | TL138002 |
| Bricket Wood M25 Junction 21 drainage pools | TL118032 |
| Bricket Wood School Lane | TL132008 |
| Bricket Wood, Winch Hill Wood | TL118030 |
| Brickfields Lake Borehamwood | TQ191959 |
| Brickground Wood Bramfield woods complex | TL278166 |
| Brickhill Green Wood Pond | SP986066 |
| Bride Hall Ayot St Laurence | TL189158 |
| Bridgedown Golf Club nr Barnet | TQ233976 |
| Briggens Hotel pond | TL412113 |
| Broad Colney  GP Lakes West | TL178035 |
| Broad Colney GP Lakes East | TL180036 |
| Broad Colney Pastures, main pool | TL179027 |
| Broad Colney pastures, small central pools | TL181030 |
| Broad Colney Pastures,small east pool | TL183031 |
| Broadfield Hall field | TL325308 |
| Broadfield Hall, house | TL323309 |
| Brocket Park | TL219125 |
| Brocket Park Cats Gallows Wood | TL217137 |
| Bromley south of Westland Green | TL412214 |
| Brookmans Park  Gobions Pond | TL252038 |
| Brookmans Park Gobions Fields | TL245035 |
| Brookmans Park Gobions new pond | TL246038 |
| Brookmans Park Gobions Oak pond | TL253036 |
| Brookmans Park Gobions tiny pond | TL247037 |
| Brookmans Park Gobions Wood lagoons | TL253035 |
| Brookman's Park Golf Club | TL247044 |
| Broxbourne Civic Hall pond | TL371082 |
| Broxbourne Deacons Field | TL368073 |
| Broxbourne Gravel Pit (NE) | TL380081 |
| Broxbourne Gravel Pit (NW) | TL376082 |
| Broxbourne Gravel Pit (SE) | TL380075 |
| Broxbourne Gravel pit (SW) | TL378072 |
| Broxbourne Gravel pit (SW) shallow pool | TL379075 |
| Broxbourne Gravel Pits | TL380070 |
| Broxbourne Wood West Car Park | TL326072 |
| Broxbourne Woods  Broad Riding Wood/ Cowheath Wood | TL344075 |
| Broxbourne Woods  Broxbourne Wood pond | TL327074 |
| Broxbourne Woods  Cowheath Wood | TL333075 |
| Broxbourne Woods  Danemead Wood  meadow | TL347080 |
| Broxbourne Woods  Danemead Wood (S) meadow | TL345079 |
| Broxbourne Woods  Highfield Wood pond | TL348084 |

| | | | |
|---|---|---|---|
| Broxbourne Woods  Hoddesdon Park Wood | TL357082 | Cheshunt Park Lake | TL352036 |
| Broxbourne Woods Box Wood | TL353093 | Childwickbury, Ladies Grove Wood | TL134092 |
| Broxbourne Woods Brambles Wood | TL336084 | Chipperfield churchyard | TL043015 |
| Broxbourne Woods HighfieldWood | TL348082 | Chipperfield Common garden pond, The | |
| Bucketsland Farm pond | TQ208986 | Brambles | TL039016 |
| Buckland ditch | TL352340 | Chipperfield Common Rose Farm Pond | TL039014 |
| Buckland, pond | TL357339 | Chipperfield Common, ponds | TL048013 |
| Bullens Green Watling Chase N | TL215061 | Chiswell Green Cuckmans Farm | TL130052 |
| Bulls Green Backlane ponds | TL274177 | Chiswell Green Royal Garden of the Rose | TL125045 |
| Bulls Lane pond Welham Green | TL239053 | Chorley Wood Common and ponds | TQ032962 |
| Bunchleys pond NW of Welham Green | TL226063 | Chorley Wood Common Church pond | TQ035965 |
| Bunkers Hill Quarry Broadgreen Wood | TL303096 | Chorley Wood Common Cottage pond | TQ031967 |
| Bunkers Lane pond | TL094060 | Chorley wood Common Little pond | TQ031966 |
| Burge End | TL144323 | Clare Hall Manor Pond, Ridge | TL219002 |
| Burleigh Bottom pond Langley | TL215218 | Clay End nr Walkern | TL304254 |
| Burleigh Farm pond, Knebworth | TL222216 | Clay Lane Farm Sawbridgeworth | TL474154 |
| Burns Green east, garden pond | TL307226 | Clothallbury Round Wood pond | TL281328 |
| Burns Green ponds | TL307225 | Codicote Lodge pond | TL214183 |
| Burns Green SW | TL305223 | Cokenach Estate, pond at entrance | TL391363 |
| Burns Green, Hebing End, pond at Pond | | Cokenach House, Lake | TL395362 |
| Cottage | TL311228 | Coldharbour Farm Pond | SP989112 |
| Burrs Green Farm S of Woodhall Park | TL326178 | Cole Green Farm | TL430312 |
| Bursteads Pond by road | TL477172 | Coles Green nr Benington | TL305241 |
| Burston Manor, Field pond | TL137037 | Colliers End Fishers Farm | TL370208 |
| Burston Manor, Moat pond | TL135037 | Colliers End Plashes Wood east | TL386203 |
| Bury Grange Farm | TL302277 | Colney Heath Lakes GP | TL203065 |
| Bury Green pond at Lower Farm | TL452211 | Combs Wood East | TL320219 |
| Bury Green ponds | TL450214 | Combs Wood nr Benington | TL318217 |
| Bury Green The Grove, new pond | TL448213 | Combs Wood west | TL317217 |
| Bury Green, Lower Farm Track | TL455207 | Commonwood Common | TL046001 |
| Bury Green, pond SW of Lower Farm | TL450206 | Coopers Green Lane/Grt Braitch Lane footpath | TL211105 |
| Bury Lake | TQ053937 | Coopers Green Lane/Hammond Lane GP | TL197103 |
| Bush Hall Hotel pond | TL238100 | Cottered Field pond | TL317286 |
| Bushey | TQ134963 | Cottered ponds | TL320294 |
| Bushey Hall Fishers Field LNR | TQ120967 | Cottered Village pond | TL316293 |
| Bushey Little Bushey Lane garden pond | TQ144957 | Cottered Warren | TL324283 |
| Bushey St James Church pond | TQ130953 | Cottered, garden ponds | TL322295 |
| Bushey, garden pond | TQ139957 | Cottered, ponds nr Berkesdongreen Spring | TL328278 |
| Butterwick Field  W seasonal ponds | TL187069 | Cottered, Rumbolds | TL325284 |
| Butterwick Field (Willow Walk) & Smallford | | Coursers Farm, pond | TL201036 |
| Water | TL429177 | Crews Hill Glasgow Gate Stud pond | TL315003 |
| Butterwick Field HCC pond | TL194067 | Crossditch 1, Kingsmead Central | TL344139 |
| Bygrave | TL268363 | Crouch Green | TL211205 |
| | | Croxley Business Park pond | TQ086952 |
| Caldecote east | TL241387 | Croxley Common Moor | TQ084946 |
| Caldecote pond by church | TL238386 | Croxley Green allotments | TQ075956 |
| Caledonian University grounds  NE | TQ135945 | Croxley Green, garden | TQ083959 |
| Capons Wood East of Chipping | TL366323 | Croxley Hall Wood | TQ079951 |
| Carpenders Park Crematorium E pond | TQ128931 | Cuffley Brook Lake | TL310019 |
| Carpenders Park Crematorium W pond | TQ126931 | Cupids Green Reservoir | TL084096 |
| Cassiobury Park NR | TQ090974 | | |
| Causeway to Tyttenhanger Farm | TL197051 | Dancers Lane pond | TQ234995 |
| Cave Bridge pond to north | TL385329 | Danesbury Park, WGC, pond | TL229170 |
| Chalk Wood pond | TL089177 | Datchworth Brookbridge Lane pond | TL269184 |
| Charlton Mill pond | TL177277 | Datchworth garden pond | TL269187 |
| Charlton Wellhead | TL176276 | Datchworth Hoppers Hall pond | TL272183 |
| Cheapside Farm Sandridge | TL152107 | de Havilland Fishing Lake, Oaklands | TL185080 |
| Chequers ditch, Welwyn Garden City | TL239114 | Digswell Lake  Digswell | TL243148 |
| Chesfield Downs Golf Centre Pond | TL237293 | Digswell Recreation ground pond | TL246148 |
| Cheshunt Park | TL348038 | Digswell, Warren Way, pond | TL247156 |
| Cheshunt Park Farm GP | TL352043 | Dilly Wood,Sacombe Green | TL349193 |

East Farm pond    TL117053

| | |
|---|---|
| East Farm pond | TL117053 |
| East Farm road pond | TL117053 |
| Edge Grove Lake nr Aldenham | TQ143989 |
| Ellenbrook, St Marks Colney Heath | TL197062 |
| Elstree Aerodrome pond | TQ164966 |
| Elstree Cemetery pond | TQ182956 |
| Elstree Golf Course NE pond | TQ181974 |
| Elstree Golf Course nr Clubhouse | TQ179969 |
| Elstree Golf Course ponds | TQ179974 |
| Ermine Street footpath | TL343001 |
| Essendon Brook | TL269083 |
| Essendon Fields S of Pinatum | TL271083 |
| Ettridge Farm pond | TL327067 |
| Exnalls & Great Hadham GC ponds | TL451195 |
| | |
| Fairlands Valley 2nd Lake | TL253243 |
| Fairlands Valley narrow pond | TL253248 |
| Fairlands Valley north pond | TL253250 |
| Fairlands Valley Park ponds | TL254244 |
| Fairlands Valley sailing lake | TL253240 |
| Fairlands Valley third lake | TL253246 |
| Fanhams Hall Ware | TL369158 |
| Felden NE roadside verge | TL049052 |
| Felden Tower Farm Pond | TL040049 |
| Feldon Howes Retreat pond | TL040049 |
| Fir & Pond Wood NR | TL280003 |
| Fir and Pond Wood, Fir Wood | TL276011 |
| Fir and Pond Wood, Pond Wood | TL279000 |
| Fir and Pond Wood, Pond Wood new ponds | TL278005 |
| Fir Tree Farm | TL321265 |
| Five Acre Wood Potters Bar | TL274015 |
| Flaunden Lower Plantation | TL020012 |
| Folly Farm Chalk pit lake Bulborne | SP943142 |
| Folly Farm ditch to west | SP865166 |
| Folly Farm pond | SP877160 |
| Forest Hill Golf Club | TL298055 |
| Friars Wood east | TL320325 |
| Frithesden Beeches | SP998108 |
| Frithesden Beeches Ashridge Estate | TL001105 |
| Frithesden Golf Course | TL004096 |
| Frogmore Hall Pit Aston | TL285205 |
| Frogmore Pits (SE) Landfill Park St GP | TL150027 |
| Frogmore Pits Lakes(NE)/R Ver Park St GP | TL150032 |
| Frogmore Pits Lakes(NW) Park St GP | TL146034 |
| Frogmore Pond Kings Walden | TL171229 |
| Furneux Pelham Corner pond | TL425290 |
| Furneux Pelham Hall pond | TL428278 |
| Furneux Pelham pond in field | TL425288 |
| Furneux Pelham roadside | TL420279 |
| Further Burydell (nr.Radlett Aerodrome) | TL153041 |
| Furze Field Wood pond in field | TL204105 |
| | |
| Gaddesden Row | TL048128 |
| Gannock Green field pond | TL318353 |
| Ganwick Corner Duke of York pond | TQ254995 |
| Gardeners End | TL318277 |
| Garston (N) Pond A | TL118009 |
| Garston, Near Chequers Lane | TL105026 |
| Gatesbury | TL393238 |
| Gatesbury Trout pool | TL393236 |
| Gilston area pond by road | TL446146 |

| | |
|---|---|
| Gilston Church | TL439137 |
| Gilston garden pond | TL438135 |
| Goffs Oak, Rosedale Lake | TL338029 |
| Grand Union Canal (GUC) and R Bulbourne | TL053058 |
| GUC Aylesbury Arm S of Puttenham | SP885138 |
| GUC Aylesbury Arm, west of Wilstone | SP899143 |
| GUC Aylesbury Arm, Wilstone | SP905143 |
| GUC Bankmill Bridge | TL008073 |
| GUC Batchworth Lock | TQ067943 |
| GUC Berkhamsted Station | SP994081 |
| GUC Bourne End & Winkwell | TL023063 |
| GUC Boxmoor Hemel Hempstead | TL053061 |
| GUC Broadway Farm to Cress Farm | TL015066 |
| GUC Bulborne to N of Marshcroft Lane | SP933137 |
| GUC Cassiobury Park Watford | TQ089974 |
| GUC Coy Carp PH | TQ041912 |
| GUC Dudswell to Lock 49 | SP972094 |
| GUC east of Lynsters Lake | TQ041916 |
| GUC east of Pynesfield Lake | TQ041907 |
| GUC Grove Golf Club | TQ086987 |
| GUC Grove Mill Lane Bridge  Watford | TQ086987 |
| GUC Hemel Hempstead W to Winkwell E | TL035062 |
| GUC Marsworth | SP927139 |
| GUC N of Hunton Bridge | TL084003 |
| GUC Nash Mills north | TL066045 |
| GUC Nash Mills South | TL071042 |
| GUC NE of Kings Langley | TL072036 |
| GUC New Ground to Cow Roast Lock | SP955108 |
| GUC NW of Abbots Langley | TL078016 |
| GUC S of Cow Roast Lock to N of Lock47 | SP961101 |
| GUC S of Croxley Common Moor | TQ075945 |
| GUC S of Kings Langley | TL077021 |
| GUC S of Lock 47 to Dudswell | SP963098 |
| GUC S of Lock 49 to Berkhamsted N | SP977088 |
| GUC S of Tring Stn to New Ground | SP951115 |
| GUC SE of Bankmill Bridge | TL008068 |
| GUC Stockers Farm | TQ050934 |
| GUC Tring Station | SP944123 |
| GUC Two Waters, Hemel Hempstead | TL057058 |
| GUC Wendover Arm Drayton Beauchamp | SP900118 |
| GUC Wendover Arm dry section Tringford Res | SP912130 |
| GUC Wendover Arm, North | SP925135 |
| GUC Wendover Arm, South, East section | SP922128 |
| GUC Wendover Arm, South, West section | SP918128 |
| GUC West of Marsworth | SP914145 |
| Gravel Pit Wood pond | TL037153 |
| Graveley small pond | TL231278 |
| Graveley Village pond | TL231278 |
| Great Bradwins Wood/Gravel Pit Wood | TL037153 |
| Great Gaddesden Marsh wood NW Home Farm | TL040117 |
| Great Gaddesden Oaken Grove | TL037114 |
| Great Groves Wood  Brickendon | TL317085 |
| Great Groves Wood, Grays pond | TL316068 |
| Great Groves Wood, Green Pond | TL320084 |
| Great Groves, Denny Dell Pond | TL318084 |
| Great Hormead Thatched Cottage | TL407302 |
| Great Offley Offley Hoo pond | TL147261 |
| Great Offley Salusbury Ave Long pond Fishing pond | TL142266 |
| Great Offley West End Farm pond | TL139275 |
| Great Pennys Farm pond | TL446146 |

| | | | |
|---|---|---|---|
| Green End, Little Munden | TL332227 | Hatfield Park Home Park & Broadwater | TL244095 |
| Green End, pond by road | TL329224 | Hatfield Park Ride | TL235093 |
| Green End, ponds in field | TL333227 | Hatfield Park Tiny Pond Milwards Park | TL237074 |
| Green Tye Village pond | TL445184 | Hatfield Pk Halfway Oak Pond 1 | TL242069 |
| Grove Golf Club | TQ085988 | Hatfield Pk Halfway Oak Pond 2 | TL243069 |
| Grubbs Lane & Kentish Lane junction | TL265056 | Hatfield Quarry pool, Sandpit Lane | TL187084 |
| Gubblecote | SP909151 | Hatfield School, west pond NWWelham Green | TL225062 |
| Gubblecote Moat | SP910151 | Hatfield Southfield School | TL227065 |
| Gustard Wood Common north | TL170150 | Hatfield Stream Woods South | TL229078 |
| Gustard Wood Common south | TL170150 | Hatfield UH de Havilland Campus balancing | |
| Gustard Wood Mid Herts Golf Course pond | | ponds | TL205085 |
| at 10th tee | TL173155 | Hatfield, Cecil Saw Mill, fishing lake | TL250098 |
| | | Hatfield, University of Hertfordshire lily pond | TL214075 |
| Haberdashers Aske GS Headmistresses pond | TQ171963 | Haultwick Langton's Lane | TL348211 |
| Haberdashers Aske School Conservation area | | Haultwick ponds | TL338233 |
| Mini Pond | TQ172964 | Hawkshead Road Pond, Brookman's Park | TL235032 |
| Haberdashers Askes School Conservation | | Hawkshead Wood | TL217027 |
| area pond Elstree | TQ172964 | Haydon Hill House lower pond | TQ126952 |
| Hadham Hall | TL457228 | Haydon Hill House pond | TQ128951 |
| Hadham Hall Douglas NR | TL453227 | Haydon Hill House upper pond | TQ128947 |
| Hadham Hall Farmers pond nr The Mound | TL454232 | Hazel Grove University of Hertfordshire | TL216072 |
| Hadham Hall Moat Pond | TL451213 | Helicon Gravel Pits, Harefield | TQ037906 |
| Hadham Hall Ponds | TL452228 | Hemel Hempstead Widmore Wood pond | TL074085 |
| Hadham Hall Willow Pond | TL452228 | Hempstead Road pond | TL115062 |
| Hadham Lodge pond | TL467221 | Henry Moore Foundation pond Widford | TL433169 |
| Hadham Mill, pond | TL429176 | Heronsgate pond | TQ024952 |
| Hailey near A10 | TL367107 | Hertford Bengeo garden pond | TL324137 |
| Haileybury College | TL357105 | Hertford Cut Kingsmead | TL344137 |
| Hall's Green ponds | TL276288 | Hertford Heath Amwell Place Farm | TL354118 |
| Hamels Park | TL377242 | Hertford Heath Amwell Place Fm Pond | TL356120 |
| Hammonds End Farm | TL121118 | Hertford Heath farmland meadows hedgerows | TL354118 |
| Hammonds End Pond Harpenden | TL124123 | Hertford Heath Goldings Wood | TL357116 |
| Hampermill Lake | TQ090944 | Hertford Heath Leafy Oak Wood | TL360119 |
| Hanbury Manor | TL348164 | Hertford Heath NR | TL349106 |
| Hanbury Manor North Lake | TL354163 | Hertford Heath NR adj Brides Pond | TL351105 |
| Hanbury Manor pond | TL353164 | Hertford Heath NR Brick ponds | TL349106 |
| Hanbury Manor, South Lake | TL353162 | Hertford Heath NR Brides Pond | TL350105 |
| Harepark Spring Wood pond | TL189165 | Hertford Heath NR Goldingtons, Crab Tree | |
| Harmer Green Village pond | TL255159 | Pond | TL354110 |
| Harmer Green Wood NE | TL253170 | Hertford Heath NR New pond | TL348105 |
| Harpenden Aldwickbury Golf Course | TL108141 | Hertford Heath NR Roundings | TL349105 |
| Harpenden Amwell Golf Course | TL165135 | Hertford Heath NR Sphagnum pond | TL348105 |
| Harpenden Common Golf Course pond | TL141122 | Hertford Heath, Garden Pond | TL354116 |
| Harpenden Common pond Harpenden | TL137137 | Hertford Hospital | TL319124 |
| Harpenden garden | TL119155 | Hertford Mandeville Road | TL326113 |
| Harpenden garden pond | TL142129 | Hertford, Ware Road, garden pond | TL344133 |
| Harpenden garden pond 2 | TL125141 | Hertingfordbury Pit | TL308113 |
| Harpenden Hospital pond | TL132156 | Hexton Mill Lane | TL114309 |
| Harpenden St Joseph's Walk Pond | TL135138 | Hexton St Faiths Well Hexton Church | TL104303 |
| Harpenden, school pond | TL135147 | High Canons, roadside pond | TQ210989 |
| Harper Lane Pits, deep pond | TL163018 | High Cross | TL363186 |
| Harper Lane Pits, small pond | TL162018 | High Cross, Rennesley Garden Wood | TL354181 |
| Harperbury Hospital grounds | TL172022 | High source of Mimram, lake | TL165225 |
| Hatfield Aerodrome channel | TL202085 | High Trees Farm Chapmore End | TL327164 |
| Hatfield Business Park, Computacenta Pond | TL215096 | High Wych | TL461147 |
| Hatfield Business Park, Fountain pond | TL213084 | High Wych, The Grove pond | TL461147 |
| Hatfield Galleria | TL216082 | Hilfield Park Reservoir (NE) | TQ161961 |
| Hatfield Park Conduit wood | TL244083 | Hilfield Park Reservoir (NW) | TQ154963 |
| Hatfield Park Dark pond Milwards | TL236065 | Hilfield Park Reservoir (SE) | TQ162957 |
| Hatfield Park Halfway Oak pond Milwards | | Hilfield Park Reservoir (SW) | TQ154955 |
| Park | TL242069 | Hilfield Park Reservoir dragonfly pond | TQ157955 |

| | |
|---|---|
| Hilfield Park Reservoir Mini pond | TQ157955 |
| Hill End Farm Langley End | TL198240 |
| Hinxworth | TL237412 |
| Hinxworth Ashwell Road | TL233407 |
| Hinxworth Place, Moat | TL239395 |
| Hitchin Coutts Fishing Lake N | TL205291 |
| Hitchin Old Wellbury | TL141297 |
| Hitchin The Willows | TL179285 |
| Hitchin, Butts Close, pond | TL181295 |
| Hitchin, Central | TL187292 |
| Hitchin, Manor Crescent, garden ponds | TL196285 |
| Hitchwood, Whitwell | TL194239 |
| Hixham Hall Lake | TL456270 |
| Hoddesdon Barclay's Park | TL368083 |
| Hoddesdon, The Meadway | TL375076 |
| Hoddesdonbury Pit south | TL355077 |
| Hoddesonbury Pit North | TL355080 |
| Hogg End Lane garden pond | TL115090 |
| Hollingson Mead Gravel Pit east Harlow | TL463123 |
| Hollingson Meads Gravel Pit west Harlow | TL456123 |
| Holmshill House Pond 2 Buckettsland Lane | TQ213991 |
| Holwell | TL165336 |
| Holwell Hyde Fishing Lake  GP Welwyn Garden City | TL264114 |
| Holwell Park Wood pond | TL273111 |
| Home Covert pond Hatfield Aerodrome | TL200089 |
| Homestalls Garden pond | TL453193 |
| Hook Wood Potters Bar | TL279016 |
| Hornbeam Common | TL345230 |
| Howe Green pond | TL285096 |
| Hunsdon House lakes, Hunsdon | TL422126 |
| Hunsdon Lords Pond | TL414122 |
| Hunsdon Moat wood | TL403138 |
| Hunsdon pond to north | TL418149 |
| Hunsdon Village pond to east | TL420142 |
| Hunsdonbury pond | TL419125 |
| Hyde Hall Farm Keyhole pond | TL342328 |
| Hyde Hill Farm pond by house | TL342327 |
| | |
| Jenningsbury Court entrance | TL313120 |
| Jenningsbury Court pond | TL341118 |
| Jersey Farm field pond  St Albans | TL177097 |
| | |
| Kelshall | TL334360 |
| Kelshall Chara field pond | TL332363 |
| Kelshall Ducks Green relict pond | TL336365 |
| Kelshall pond nr Church | TL329360 |
| Kelshall track to south | TL331359 |
| Kelshall,  Kelshall Street garden pond | TL332362 |
| Kendal Wood pond | TQ171983 |
| Kettle Green,  Brands Farm ponds | TL417189 |
| Kimpton Mill pond | TL198185 |
| Kings Langley AC Fishing Lake | TL075035 |
| Kings Langley Churchyard | TL073024 |
| Kings Langley Common north | TL065032 |
| Kings Langley Common south | TL065028 |
| Kings Langley Fishery Lake | TL077023 |
| Kings Mead Sweet Mead | TL343140 |
| Kings Waldenbury Lake Confidential Site | TL161234 |
| Kingsmead Floods Chadwell Mead | TL348137 |
| Kingsmead Sweet Mead | TL346137 |

| | |
|---|---|
| Kingsmeads Cattle pond | TL338138 |
| Kingsmeads NR | TL343136 |
| Kingsmeads West Pool | TL348137 |
| Kitts End Cottage pond | TQ245985 |
| Kitwells pond  Borehamwood | TQ192992 |
| Knebworth Park NE, long pond | TL230214 |
| Knebworth Park NW | TL226213 |
| Knebworth Park SW | TL220209 |
| | |
| Lady Grove garden pond Kiln Wood | TL186243 |
| Lamer Park | TL185151 |
| Langley Lodge pond | TL063015 |
| Langtons Lane E of Dane End | TL347212 |
| Latchford Trout Lake | TL388210 |
| Lea Valley Park Bowyers Water | TL367015 |
| Lea Valley Park Cheshunt Gravel Pits South | TL370020 |
| Lea Valley Park Cheshunt Pits Turnford | TL370030 |
| Lea Valley Park Dobbs Weir | TL384082 |
| Lea Valley Park east of Bowyers Water | TL369016 |
| Lea Valley Park Friday Lake | TL370018 |
| Lea Valley Park Marsh Bridge | TL371011 |
| Lea Valley Park North Met Pit NE | TL370031 |
| Lea Valley Park North Met Pit SE | TL370029 |
| Lea Valley Park North Met Pit W | TL369039 |
| Lea Valley Park Silvermeade NR North Broxbourne | TL372063 |
| Lea Valley Park Silvermeade NR South | TL372059 |
| Lea Valley Park Thistly Marsh NE | TL367021 |
| Lea Valley Park Turnford Marsh Turnford & Cheshunt pits | TL369043 |
| Lea Valley Park Turnford Marsh, Slipe Lane Pits | TL372046 |
| Lea Valley Park Wharfe Lane | TL367036 |
| Lea Valley Park, Small lake, Turnford Brook | TL369038 |
| Leasey Bridge lake to west | TL157147 |
| Lemsford Brocket Park | TL219125 |
| Lemsford Mill pond | TL219123 |
| Lemsford Springs | TL223120 |
| Lemsford Springs, Garden pond | TL223122 |
| Letchmore Heath pond, grounds of Hare Krishna temple | TQ152977 |
| Letchmore Heath Village pond | TQ153976 |
| Letchworth Business Park | TL232331 |
| Letchworth Hall Hotel | TL216307 |
| Letchworth Kingfisher Court garden pond | TL211341 |
| Letchworth Pix Brook | TL209341 |
| Letchworth Sewage Works | TL208342 |
| Letchworth, Norton Common | TL218335 |
| Letchworth, Wilbury | TL201325 |
| Letty Green Deadfield Lane | TL276107 |
| Levens Green site to west | TL350225 |
| Ley Green pond | TL156244 |
| Libury Hall, Great Munden | TL345235 |
| Lilley Hoo Lane | TL125269 |
| Lilley roadside pond | TL117268 |
| Lilley Stockinghill Plantation | TL123275 |
| Lilley Village pond | TL118264 |
| Little Berkhamsted  Stockings Lane pond | TL301088 |
| Little Gaddesden pond | SP995130 |
| Little Gaddesden village pond | SP997128 |
| Little Hadham, Muggins Wood | TL443219 |

Little Hormead Glebe House pond — TL405289
Little Hyde Hall — TL505153
Little Kendal's Farm footpath pond — TQ164981
Little Offley Pond — TL129285
Lockleys Wood N — TL248160
Long Leys Farm ditch to north — SP891166
Long Marston Marstongate Farm — SP886167
Long Marston Old Church Cottage Garden — SP894156
Long Marston Pond, nr school — SP896156
Long Marston stream to South — SP894153
Long Marston, Chapel Lane Moat — SP894156
Luffenhall nr Cromer, Manor Farm — TL293287
Lye Lane Garden pond — TL134023
Lyle End Farm pond — TL334322
Lyle End Farm, Wood — TL330317

Mackerye End — TL160163
Mackerye End Farm Harpenden — TL158147
Malcolm Barker Fishing Lake S of Bishops Stortford — TL493199
Manifold Ditch east Kingsmead — TL347142
Manifold Ditch west Kingsmead — TL344139
Manifold ditch, Kings Mead Hertford — TL344139
Manor Groves Hotel — TL459147
Maple Lodge LNR — TQ036924
Mardlebury Manor Farm pond Reed End — TL352365
Mardlebury Manor Reed End — TL351365
Mardlebury Pond, Datchworth — TL260185
Mardlebury, pond by road Reed End — TL350364
Mardley Heath — TL246183
Mardley Heath pond — TL246183
Markyate area S of Pepperstock — TL080177
Markyate NE of village — TL070169
Marshalls Heath north — TL162150
Marshalls Heath south — TL161148
Marshland wood pond Widford — TL428152
Marsworth Moat Farm — SP917148
Mathams Wood east — TL463184
Maydencroft Aquatics St Ippolitts — TL185271
Maydencroft Manor Ponds — TL183275
Meesden — TL427325
Meesden, Lower Green, garden pond — TL421331
Meesden, Lower Green, pond — TL421331
Mentley Farm — TL375236
Mentley Lane — TL383237
Mentmore south woodland edge — SP902183
Merry Hill pond A — TQ136937
Merry Hill Pond C — TQ137940
Mill Green Golf Club, Footpath Pond 1 — TL242100
Mill Green Golf Club, Gipsy Lane Field — TL249104
Mill Green Golf Club, Pond 2, Tee 7 — TL244102
Mill Green Golf Club, Pond 3 — TL244103
Mill Green Golf Club, Pond 4 — TL247105
Mill Green Golf Club, Pond 5, Tee 12 — TL258104
Mill Green Golf Club, Pond 6 — TL257103
Mill Green Golf Club, Pond 7 — TL259103
Mill Green Golf Club, Pond 8, Clubhouse — TL247101
Mill Green Golf Club, WGC — TL245103
Millhouse Farm garden pond — TL108035
Millhouse Farm pond — TL108035
Mimmshall Brook Saffron Green — TQ222977

Mimmshall Brook, Abdale House — TL230038
Mimmshall Brook, Wash Lane Common — TL231005
Mole Wood Waterford — TL317146
Monks Wood, Stevenage — TL245235
Moor Green pond by Roman Road — TL323271
Moor Green, ditch by road — TL326262
Moor Hall ponds, Moor Green — TL327269
Moor Mill GP, north pools — TL145033
Moor Mill, SW pools — TL142026
Moor Mill, west pools — TL143030
Moor Park Golf Club pond 1 — TQ076928
Moor Park Golf Club pond 2 — TQ077930
Morley Hall garden pond — TL387155
Morley Hall near Wareside — TL387154
Much Hadham Daneswood — TL433187
Much Hadham east — TL431194
Much Hadham New Barns Farm — TL419198
Much Hadham south — TL428187
Munches Wood, lake — TL296315
Munden Spring — TL128001
Mundenbury Church — TL355242
Mundenbury pond in field — TL352245
Mutfords — TL399284

Near Breachwood Green — TL142208
New Hall Farm Babbs Green — TL389163
New Lake east — TL421358
New Lake west — TL419358
New Park Pond Northaw — TL286019
New River Stanstead Abbotts — TL379118
New River, Admirals Walk — TL375083
New River, Kingsmead — TL347139
New River, Theobalds's Park — TL348008
Newnham Manor Farm — TL243377
Newton Wood east — TL230223
Newton Wood west — TL225225
Nicky Line, N of Redbourn — TL114129
Nicky Line, S of Harpenden — TL114135
Noahs Ark NE of Ware — TL378159
Nobland Green area — TL405175
Nobles Farm — TL362246
Nomansland — TL171125
Norfolk Lodge Pond — TQ242994
North Mymms near Church — TL220042
North Mymms Park Hawkshead Wood — TL221032
North Mymms Park Set aside — TL216036
North Mymms Park, Cangsley Grove N — TL217034
North Mymms Park, Cangsley Grove S, large pond — TL219033
North Mymms, pond near church — TL220045
North Mymms, pond to North, Tollgate Rd — TL221048
Northaw Brook Burnt Farm — TL316011
Northaw Brook Soper's Viaduct — TL307017
Northaw garden pond The Ridgeway — TL286037
Northaw Great Wood pond — TL281038
Northaw Great Wood, Country Park — TL282042
Northaw Great Wood, Cuffley Camp — TL295043
Northaw Valley Pond — TL284015
Northaw, village pond — TL277024
Northchurch Common — SP978116
Northey Wood — TL403331

| | |
|---|---|
| Northfield Grange open ground | SP945128 |
| Norton Green Meadow | TL227229 |
| Norton Green Pond | TL229234 |
| Norton Green, Burleigh Meadows | TL221231 |
| Norton, pond | TL227342 |
| Notley Green Lane E of Sandon | TL333348 |
| | |
| Oaklands College ornamental pond | TL181075 |
| Oaklands college small pond | TL191075 |
| Oaklands Welwyn Garden pond | TL244175 |
| Oakmere Pak Potters Bar | TL264013 |
| Old Claypits Farm White Stubbs Lane | TL311068 |
| Old Manor Farm | TL408378 |
| Old Parkbury GP | TL163025 |
| Orchid Pit and Fishing Lake  Sandpit Lane GP | TL186082 |
| Orchid Pit Smallford | TL186081 |
| Otterspool, floodplain pools | TQ128990 |
| Oughtenhead Common | TL167303 |
| Oxhey | TQ116938 |
| Oxhey Woods LNR Watford | TQ107923 |
| | |
| Pann Mill Cottages Fishing Lake | TL194203 |
| Panshanger (Black Fan) Lagoon  Welwyn Garden City | TL254137 |
| Panshanger Park GP Lake Poplars Green | TL282131 |
| Panshanger Park SW | TL281127 |
| Park Wood, Ragged Hall Lane | TL127052 |
| Parkfield Park Potters Bar large pond | TL261014 |
| Patchetts Green temporary ponds | TQ139976 |
| Patmore Heath Bogs Cottage pond | TL449254 |
| Patmore Heath Bogs Wood | TL453253 |
| Patmore Heath NR | TL443257 |
| Patmore Heath NR Centre pond | TL443257 |
| Patmore Heath NR Pennies pond | TL442255 |
| Patmore Heath NR Twin ponds | TL443258 |
| Perry Green | TL437178 |
| Perry Green garden pond | TL437174 |
| Perry Green roadside pond | TL440161 |
| Peters Green Lawrence End Park | TL143194 |
| Peters Green roadside verge | TL147202 |
| Philpotts Wood, Sandon | TL326349 |
| Pirton footpath | TL145315 |
| Pirton Hall | TL126328 |
| Pirton Toot Hill Moat | TL147316 |
| Pirton Village Pond | TL146316 |
| Pishiobury stream Rowneybury | TL477132 |
| Pitstone Hill Quarry | SP943142 |
| Plaistowes Farm pond | TL119046 |
| Pole Hole Farm pond | TL454127 |
| Pole Hole Gravel Pits | TL456126 |
| Pollard Wood Quarry | TL299096 |
| Pond adj GUC S of Puttenham | SP885138 |
| Potten End village pond | TL017088 |
| Potters Bar Dame Alice Owen School | TL242006 |
| Potters Bar Morven Park pond | TL262017 |
| Potters Bar, Fieldview, garden | TL253006 |
| Potters Green | TL352208 |
| Potwells, near Ridge | TL215030 |
| Poynders End Farm pond | TL191247 |
| Pre Hotel south St Albans | TL132079 |
| Priorswood Clematis | TL376144 |

| | |
|---|---|
| Private site | TL140190 |
| Private site 1 | TL219263 |
| Private Site 2 | TL140190 |
| Puttenham fields | SP884159 |
| Puttenham NW ditch | SP887156 |
| Puttocks End Cottages | TL418317 |
| Pye Corner | TL449121 |
| Pynesfield Lake | TQ037912 |
| | |
| Quickswood Farm | TL278328 |
| | |
| R Gade Piccotts End Garden Centre | TL047096 |
| R Lea above weir Amwell Magna | TL379129 |
| Rabley Heath ponds | TL238188 |
| Rabley Heath, garden pond | TL235193 |
| Radwell | TL227356 |
| Radwell east Icknield Way | TL247357 |
| Raffin Green Farm ponds | TL275195 |
| Red House Farm | SP886161 |
| Redbourn Golf Course North | TL107141 |
| Redbourn Golf Course South, Pond | TL108139 |
| Redcoats Pond | TL208266 |
| Redwell Wood | TL217026 |
| Redwoods Garden pond, WGC | TL238151 |
| Reed Driftway | TL363358 |
| Reed Goodfellows pond | TL361361 |
| Reed old fish pond | TL365358 |
| Reed pond by PH | TL364361 |
| Reed Rokey wood | TL374358 |
| Rib Valley Lakes, North | TL336157 |
| Rib Valley Lakes, South | TL335155 |
| Rickneys Quarry | TL318153 |
| Ridge, Garden pond SE of village | TL219002 |
| Rigery pond, Standon Green End | TL362207 |
| River Ash  Widfordbury | TL413163 |
| River Ash Amwell Quarry | TL377132 |
| River Ash Easeneye Estate (NE) | TL384143 |
| River Ash Easeneye Estate (SE) | TL380139 |
| River Ash Easeneye Estate E | TL376134 |
| River Ash Hadham Cross | TL430186 |
| River Ash Hadham Cross S | TL428180 |
| River Ash Mardocks Farm | TL393147 |
| River Ash Wareside east | TL403157 |
| River Ash Wareside west | TL399152 |
| River Beane Aston pumping stn ford pond | TL281234 |
| River Beane Cromer | TL296281 |
| River Beane Frogmore Hall | TL285204 |
| River Beane Goldings South | TL313136 |
| River Beane Hartham Common | TL328134 |
| River Beane Hertford North | TL317130 |
| River Beane HolbrookFarm bridge | TL280226 |
| River Beane nr Holbrook Farm | TL284221 |
| River Beane Stapleford (N) | TL314175 |
| River Beane Stapleford (S) | TL315164 |
| River Beane Stevenage | TL280230 |
| River Beane Walkern ford | TL292265 |
| River Beane Waterford Marsh | TL314147 |
| River Beane Watton at Stone Mill Lane | TL301195 |
| River Beane White Hall Farm | TL287215 |
| River Beane Woodhall Park (N) | TL310189 |
| River Beane Woodhall Park (S) | TL316182 |

| Location | Grid Ref |
|---|---|
| River Beane, Whitehall pump stn 3, pond | TL285220 |
| River Bulbourne Hemel Hempstead W to Winkwell | TL035063 |
| River Bulbourne S of Dudswell | SP950093 |
| River Chess Batchworth | TQ078942 |
| River Chess Frogmore Meadows Chenies Bottom | TQ022988 |
| River Chess Hampermill Lake | TQ093942 |
| River Chess nr Solesbridge Mill Chorleywood | TQ043968 |
| River Chess Sarratt Bottom | TQ032991 |
| River Chess Sarratt Mill Bridge | TQ036978 |
| River Colne London Colney | TL183037 |
| River Colne & Colney Heath Common | TL201059 |
| River Colne A41 Watford | TQ125985 |
| River Colne Batchworth Lake | TQ056953 |
| River Colne Bricket Wood E | TL139012 |
| River Colne Bricket Wood S | TQ133998 |
| River Colne Bury Lake | TQ049939 |
| River Colne Bushey Hall Farm | TQ118975 |
| River Colne Bushey Mill Bridge | TQ119981 |
| River Colne by Tyttenhanger House | TL189047 |
| River Colne Church Lane, Colney Heath | TL199059 |
| River Colne Colney Street | TL157018 |
| River Colne Coy Carp PH | TQ041912 |
| River Colne Hampermill Lake | TQ093942 |
| River Colne Little Munden Farm | TL138008 |
| River Colne Moynihans Field | TL429177 |
| River Colne Munden House Ford | TL137004 |
| River Colne North Mymms Park | TL219046 |
| River Colne North of Water Lane Watford | TQ117967 |
| River Colne nr London Colney | TL166030 |
| River Colne Old Parkbury | TL161021 |
| River Colne Old Parkbury south | TL161019 |
| River Colne Otterspool | TQ128995 |
| River Colne Oxhey Park, West Watford | TQ114954 |
| River Colne Pynesfield Lake | TQ037907 |
| River Colne Riverside Road Recreation Ground | TQ107953 |
| River Colne Stockers Lake, Rickmansworth | TQ049939 |
| River Colne Tyttenhager GP central | TL191048 |
| River Colne Tyttenhanger GP north | TL193052 |
| River Colne Tyttenhanger GP south | TL189045 |
| River Colne Watford | TQ117967 |
| River Gade  Piccotts End | TL049092 |
| River Gade  Water End | TL039104 |
| River Gade Cassiobury Park | TQ091967 |
| River Gade Croxley Common Moor NE | TQ081951 |
| River Gade Croxley Common Moor SW | TQ075946 |
| River Gade Grt Gaddesden North | TL025124 |
| River Gade HMWT Reserve Cassiobury Park | TQ089974 |
| River Gade Hudnall Corner | TL013133 |
| River Gade Kings Langley South | TL076020 |
| River Gade small stream Cassiobury Park | TQ089969 |
| River Gade Water End weir | TL040102 |
| River Gade Watford Watercress Beds NR | TQ090969 |
| River Gade, Great Gaddesdon East | TL031111 |
| River Hiz Cadwell | TL188324 |
| River Hiz Ickleford | TL185314 |
| River Hiz near clay pit | TL180350 |
| River Hiz nr Old Ramerick | TL181350 |
| River Hiz Old Ramerick | TL179348 |
| River Ivel Norton Mill | TL237351 |
| River Ivel, Radwell | TL232354 |
| River Lea  Mill Green (West) Hatfield | TL239099 |
| River Lea Amwell . | TL374133 |
| River Lea Amwell, backwater 'lake' | TL374131 |
| River Lea at Holycross Lake Amwell | TL374132 |
| River Lea Batford Springs | TL146150 |
| River Lea below weir Amwell Magna | TL380127 |
| River Lea Broxbourne | TL376066 |
| River Lea Broxbourne GP east | TL381071 |
| River Lea Broxbourne GP west | TL375070 |
| River Lea East Hyde | TL129171 |
| River Lea Grays Wood Wheathampstead | TL195139 |
| River Lea Harpenden North | TL133165 |
| River Lea Hertford FC south | TL321121 |
| River Lea Kings Mead Central | TL345138 |
| River Lea Kings Mead East | TL345141 |
| River Lea Kings Mead West | TL337137 |
| River Lea Leasey Bridge Lane | TL162144 |
| River Lea Marford Farm Wheathampstead | TL187142 |
| River Lea Marquis of Granby Harpenden | TL148149 |
| River Lea Mill Green (East) Hatfield | TL249097 |
| River Lea N of Piggottshill Wood | TL152148 |
| River Lea Nav Stanstead Abbotts | TL383115 |
| River Lea Navigation  Amwell | TL374126 |
| River Lea Navigation Cheshunt Junction | TL369022 |
| River Lea Navigation Cheshunt Lake | TL370031 |
| River Lea Navigation Cheshunt Lock | TL373035 |
| River Lea Navigation Kings Weir | TL373051 |
| River Lea Navigation Marsh Bridge | TL372009 |
| River Lea Navigation Slipe Lane | TL372047 |
| River Lea Navigation Stanstead Lock | TL381122 |
| River Lea Navigation Waltham Common Lock | TL370019 |
| River Lea Navigation Wharfe Road | TL373054 |
| River Lea near Black Bridge  Wheathampstead | TL190143 |
| River Lea Small River Lea Cadmore Lane | TL367027 |
| River Lea Small River Lea Cheshunt Marsh Lea Valley Park | TL369005 |
| River Lea Small River Lea Marsh Bridge Cheshunt | TL370010 |
| River Lea Small River Lea Thistly Marsh south | TL367021 |
| River Lea Stanborough Lake | TL228108 |
| River Lea Stanborough Reed Marsh | TL230105 |
| River Lea The Wash Hertford | TL328127 |
| River Lea Ware | TL364143 |
| River Lea Ware SE | TL368138 |
| River Lea Ware West | TL352143 |
| River Lea Water End | TL202140 |
| River Lea Water Hall Quarry | TL298097 |
| River Lea weir N of Water Hall | TL303103 |
| River Lea west of Wheathampstead | TL175145 |
| River Lea Wheathampstead | TL183142 |
| River Lea Woodhall Farm Hatfield | TL239101 |
| River Lynch  Admirals Walk | TL382082 |
| River Mimram Bessemer Rd to Digswell Water | TL243153 |
| River Mimram Church Path | TL176218 |
| River Mimram Codicote Bottom to Fulling Mill | TL200160 |
| River Mimram Codicote pumping station | TL211175 |
| River Mimram Digswell Water to Tewin Water | TL255145 |
| River Mimram Fulling Mill to Singlers Marsh | TL225168 |
| River Mimram Kimpton Ford to Codicote Bottom | TL205183 |

| | |
|---|---|
| River Mimram Kimpton Mill | TL197185 |
| River Mimram Lockleys to Bessamer Rd | TL236155 |
| River Mimram Panshanger Park east | TL302122 |
| River Mimram Poplars Green Welwyn Garden City | TL278134 |
| River Mimram Tewin Water to Tewinbury Fm | TL264140 |
| River Mimram Tewinbury Fm to Poplars Green | TL270137 |
| River Mimram, Panshanger Park, Broadwater | TL293125 |
| River Mimram, Tewinbury Reserve | TL263140 |
| River Mimram, Tewinwater lake | TL253147 |
| River Mimram/ R.Lea confluence | TL319122 |
| River Oughten, Oughtenhead | TL168304 |
| River Quin, north of Dassels | TL394295 |
| River Rhee Ashwell End | TL254415 |
| River Rhee Dunton Lodge | TL259438 |
| River Rhee Whitegate Bridge | TL264440 |
| River Rib Standon | TL394212 |
| River Rib Barwick Ford north | TL385191 |
| River Rib Braughing dismantled railway, Gatesbury | TL391238 |
| River Rib Cold Christmas | TL374173 |
| River Rib Hamel's Mead | TL386247 |
| River Rib Hanging Wood | TL386199 |
| River Rib Latchford (NW) | TL388210 |
| River Rib Latchford North | TL393207 |
| River Rib Paynes Hall | TL338163 |
| River Rib Rib Valley Lakes | TL336158 |
| River Rib, Aspenden | TL362285 |
| River Rib, Thundridge | TL369174 |
| River Stort  Pishiobury Park, Sawbridgeworth | TL485139 |
| River Stort Bishops Stortford N Central | TL489223 |
| River Stort Bishops Stortford Central | TL489217 |
| River Stort Bishops Stortford E | TL494202 |
| River Stort Bishops Stortford N | TL491224 |
| River Stort Bishops Stortford NE | TL490211 |
| River Stort Bishops Stortford SE | TL496193 |
| River Stort Bishops Stortford SE Twyford Lock | TL492191 |
| River Stort Bishops Stortford W | TL489208 |
| River Stort Moorhen PH | TL447117 |
| River Stort N of Kecksys Bridge | TL491158 |
| River Stort Navigation Harlow NE | TL460120 |
| River Stort Navigation Hollingson Meads | TL457121 |
| River Stort Navigation Rowneybury nr Sawbridgeworth | TL477130 |
| River Stort Navigation S of Spelbrook Lock | TL491175 |
| River Stort Navigation Sawbridgeworth NE | TL487152 |
| River Stort Navigation Tednambury Farm | TL491162 |
| River Stort nr Roydon Lock | TL413106 |
| River Stort Old Harlow | TL476129 |
| River Stort Parndon Mead | TL430113 |
| River Stort Redericks | TL466128 |
| River Stort Sawbridgeworth Reed Marsh | TL491158 |
| River Stort Sawbridgeworth SE | TL488145 |
| River Stort south of Pye Corner Harlow | TL453119 |
| River Stort Thorley Street north | TL496193 |
| River Ver  Park Street  St.Albans | TL149045 |
| River Ver  St.Albans (NW) | TL136077 |
| River Ver Bow Bridge | TL128087 |
| River Ver Friars Wash | TL087148 |
| River Ver Redbourn south | TL109118 |
| River Ver Redbournbury Mill | TL118109 |

| | |
|---|---|
| River Ver Redbournbury north | TL118110 |
| River Ver Redbournbury South | TL121107 |
| River Ver Shafford Farm | TL125095 |
| River Ver Sopwell North | TL155052 |
| River Ver Sopwell South | TL153047 |
| River Ver, Drop Lane | TL148015 |
| River Ver, Moor Mill Inn | TL151023 |
| River Ver, Park St GP | TL150031 |
| River Ver, Smug Oak Lane | TL150023 |
| River Ver, St Albans Watercress LNR | TL153063 |
| Roe End Farm pond | TL045157 |
| Roe End Lane west | TL035162 |
| Roe Green | TL316337 |
| Rolls Wood pond | TL265120 |
| Rolls Wood Pond south | TL265119 |
| Roman Footpath nr Moor Hall | TL325274 |
| Roman Road nr Frenchcroft Wood E of Gardners End | TL323271 |
| Rothamsted Expl Stn Lily pond | TL135135 |
| Rothamsted Expl Stn Reservoir | TL118137 |
| Roundhill Wood | SP938089 |
| Roundhill Wood north | SP938091 |
| Rowley Green NR Borehamwood | TQ216960 |
| Rowneybury | TL473133 |
| Roydon mill GP | TL401104 |
| Rudwick Hall Pond | TL148197 |
| Rushden Green fpth to South | TL312302 |
| Rye End Farm pond Kimpton | TL196189 |
| Rye House Marsh | TL385105 |
| Rye House Station Hoddesdon | TL386098 |
| Rye Meads | TL392107 |
| Rye Meads  Eastern Lakes | TL392106 |
| Rye Meads NR | TL385108 |
| Rye Meads, North Lagoons | TL385104 |
| Rye Meads, The Meadows | TL388106 |
| Rye Meads Marsh | TL398105 |
| Sacombe Green Lowgate Lane | TL352201 |
| Sacombe Lakes | TL335186 |
| Sacombe Park | TL344182 |
| Sacombe Park, Church Wood pond | TL342194 |
| Sacombe Park, Home Farm Pond | TL341191 |
| Sacombe Park, Low Wood Pond | TL344193 |
| Sacombe Park, Meadow nr Garden House | TL348188 |
| Sacombe Park, Red House pond | TL342191 |
| Saffron Green | TQ210970 |
| Sandridge,Langley Grove garden pond | TL174106 |
| Sandridgebury | TL162107 |
| Sarratt pond by Cricketer's PH | TQ043993 |
| Sawtrees Farm south of Barwick Ford | TL388180 |
| Scales Park East | TL422333 |
| Scales Park nr Anstey | TL415334 |
| Scatterdells Wood pond | TL056029 |
| SE of Langley | TL220221 |
| Shafford Mill pond | TL125088 |
| Shenley allotments pond | TQ192999 |
| Shenley Dover Green round pond | TL202013 |
| Shenley Fishing Pool, Dover Green | TL203011 |
| Shenley village 'Cage' pond | TL189007 |
| Shenley, edge of wood N of Stud Farm | TL195016 |
| Shenley, pond, Col. Wild's Wood | TL194007 |

| | | | |
|---|---|---|---|
| Shenleybury | TL181019 | Stevenage Ashtree Wood | TL258241 |
| Sherrards Park Wood WGC | TL228140 | Stevenage Box Wood East | TL270266 |
| Shirelane Farm | SP932077 | Stevenage Box Wood West | TL268264 |
| Silver Hill Roadside pond | TQ202989 | Stevenage Brook, Long Meadow, Astonbury | |
| Silver Hill woodland pond  Borehamwood | TQ198992 | Wood | TL276207 |
| Slate Hall Farm reservoir | TL343338 | Stevenage Canterbury Way | TL247264 |
| Smallford garden old small pond | TL198073 | Stevenage Chell's Manor pond | TL267253 |
| Smallford garden ponds | TL198073 | Stevenage Golf Club | TL269221 |
| Smallford Lake nr. St.Albans | TL197071 | Stevenage GSK | TL236225 |
| Solebridge Water Gardens | TQ043972 | Stevenage GSK Res Centre art lake & river | TL239222 |
| Solesbridge Mill Water Gardens | TQ043966 | Stevenage GSK site | TL236225 |
| Soutfields School grounds | TL226065 | Stevenage Herts Outdoors | TL248251 |
| South Lodge Sacombe Green | TL353203 | Stevenage Serpentine Close pond | TL263268 |
| South Mimms  Swanland road lagoons | TL232026 | Stevenage Three Horshoes PH pond | TL276207 |
| South Mimms Packhorse Lane | TL206019 | Stockers Lake E, Rickmansworth | TQ051934 |
| South Mimms Wash Lane Common, Mimms | | Stockers Lake W, Rickmansworth | TQ045935 |
| Pond | TL232002 | Stocking Pelham NW Conservation path &pond | TL440294 |
| South Mimms, Five Bells Farm Pond, | | Stocking Pelham sub-station NR. | TL454286 |
| Bridgefoot | TL232006 | Stocking Pelham, lake nr Church | TL449292 |
| South of Gaddesden Row | TL046104 | Stonebury Farm | TL385281 |
| Southern Green pond  Rushden | TL311318 | Sutes north of High Cross | TL366190 |
| Southfields Farm Throcking | TL331306 | Swades Farm E of Ware | TL382149 |
| Spellbrook Farm pond | TL483179 | Swallow Grove Farm, Hertford | TL335109 |
| Spring Oak Bushes | TL418357 | Symondshyde Farm pond | TL199114 |
| Squires Lake  Borehamwood | TQ185987 | Symondshyde Farm pond in field | TL200114 |
| St Albans Abbey View Road garden pond | TL142073 | Symondshyde Great Wood | TL198113 |
| St Albans Belsize Close Jersey Farm | TL174097 | Symondshyde Great Wood South | TL199107 |
| St Albans Boissy Park | TL184070 | | |
| St Albans Grebe House pond | TL136073 | Tea Green Village pond | TL136230 |
| St Albans Hazelwood Drive | TL172074 | Telegraph Hill Hexton | TL117288 |
| St Albans Jersey Farm Woodland Park NW | TL169100 | Telegraph Hill HMWT Reserve | TL122289 |
| St Albans Kingshill Ave | TL166089 | Tewin | TL265157 |
| St Albans Marshals Drive | TL162088 | Tewin Close Tewin Wood pond | TL264164 |
| St Albans Milford Close | TL178093 | Tewin Garden | TL266146 |
| St Albans Riverside AC | TL154062 | Tewin Hill pond | TL274153 |
| St Albans Riverside Road garden pond | TL153064 | Tewin Orchard pond | TL268156 |
| St Albans Salisbury Ave | TL167075 | Tewin Upper Green ponds | TL271155 |
| St Albans Sandpit Lane | TL170082 | Tharbies Pond by road | TL470162 |
| St Albans Sherwood Avenue | TL169089 | The Brook  Borehamwood (S) | TQ187978 |
| St Albans Springwood Walk | TL176086 | The Brook  Borehamwood(N) | TQ184981 |
| St Albans St Stephens open space pond | TL143059 | The Commons  Welwyn Garden City | TL252105 |
| St Albans Verulam Golf Club | TL155063 | The Node ponds Codicote | TL215199 |
| St Albans Verulamium Lake large lake NE | TL140070 | Theobalds Park College Lake | TL349008 |
| St Albans Verulamium Park large Lake NW | TL139073 | Thieves Lane, Hertford | TL306124 |
| St Albans Wildlife Watercress LNR | TL153063 | Thorley Church Pond | TL476188 |
| St Albans, Sewell Close | TL181072 | Thorley Flood Pound | TL491186 |
| St Edmunds College Old Hall Green | TL367218 | Thorley Wood | TL488185 |
| St Ibbs Lake Hitchin | TL196267 | Three Valleys Water Treatment Works, pond, | |
| St Margarets Farm pond G Gaddesden | TL018117 | Clay Lane, Bushey | TQ155943 |
| St Pauls Waldenbury Lake at the Bury | TL190217 | Throcking Hall pond | TL338300 |
| Stagenhoe Lake Chalkleys Wood | TL185225 | Throcking New Barn | TL338301 |
| Stanborough Lake NE Welwyn Garden City | TL228111 | Thunderidgehill Cowards | TL370169 |
| Standalone Farm, Letchwoth | TL209338 | Thundridge Hill | TL368168 |
| Standon | TL414205 | Tillers End Farm pond in field | TL364259 |
| Standon Lodge Lake | TL405208 | Titmore Green Pond | TL214265 |
| Standon Lodge north | TL401212 | Titmore Green, Lawn Pond | TL216266 |
| Stanstead Abbots Gravel Pit (SE) | TL393107 | TL10G | TL123029 |
| Stanstead Abbotts Gravel Pit (SW) | TL388110 | TL13A | TL100300 |
| Stanstead Abbotts Gravel Pit North | TL388110 | TL13F | TL120300 |
| Stanstead Mill Stream Amwell Magna | TL380126 | TL13G | TL120320 |
| Stanstead Mill Stream Stanstead Abbotts | TL384115 | TL13R | TL160320 |

| | |
|---|---|
| TL13S | TL160340 |
| TL13W | TL180320 |
| TL30R | TL360020 |
| TL31P | TL349186 |
| TL32D | TL309263 |
| Toto's Way, N of Widford | TL421168 |
| TQ19D | TQ110974 |
| TQ19J | TQ122988 |
| Tring Bridleway | SP912105 |
| Tring Memorial Gardens Ornamental Pond | SP927114 |
| Tring Morefields garden pond | SP924124 |
| Tring Park, Road Sump lagoon | SP928109 |
| Tring Reservoirs Marsworth Reservoir | SP922137 |
| Tring Reservoirs Tringford Reservoir | SP917135 |
| Tring Reservoirs Wilstone Reservoir Drayton Beauchamp | SP903128 |
| Tring Reservoirs Wilstone reservoir Wilstone | SP903130 |
| Tring Reservoirs Startops Reservoir east | SP921137 |
| Tring Reservoirs Startops reservoir west | SP917137 |
| Tring Reservoirs Wilstone Reservoir east corner | SP910132 |
| Tring, Boarscroft Farm ponds | SP875164 |
| Tring, garden,Longbridge Close | SP925128 |
| Trowley Bottom Farm | TL077138 |
| Turnford, garden | TL373003 |
| Tykes Water, Radlett | TQ173987 |
| Tykeswater Lake Elstree | TQ173963 |
| Tykeswater tributary ditch Little Kendals | TQ169980 |
| Tyttenhanger Farm | TL190040 |
| Tyttenhanger Farm, ditch | TL197050 |
| Tyttenhanger Green Cell Barnes House Pond Highfield Park | TL171058 |
| Tyttenhanger Green Highfield Park East | TL173057 |
| Tyttenhanger Green Highfield Park West | TL170055 |
| Tyttenhanger Green Little Green garden ponds | TL178059 |
| Tyttenhanger Green, Highfield Lane pond | TL181049 |
| Tyttenhanger Green, Little Green, Wild pond | TL178059 |
| Tyttenhanger Lakes GP | TL192059 |
| Valley Road open space pond | TL225125 |
| Venus Hill Austins Hall Fm pond | TL016016 |
| Venus Hill Mauldens pond | TL013018 |
| Wakeley Farm pond behind farm | TL342268 |
| Wakeley Farm pond by road | TL346267 |
| Wakeley Farm pond in field | TL343270 |
| Walkern Dovecot pond | TL289265 |
| Walkern Hall Farm, west pond | TL298250 |
| Walkernbury Farm | TL305262 |
| Wall Hall bridge over stream | TQ134996 |
| Wall Hall Campus | TQ138994 |
| Wallington Common NR Coles Wood pond | TL293326 |
| Wallington Meadows pond 1 | TL283334 |
| Wallington pond by Pond cottage | TL293336 |
| Walsworth Recreation Ground pond | TL187301 |
| Wandon End pond | TL136224 |
| Wandon Green Farm | TL145205 |
| Wants End farm pond | TL162245 |
| Ware garden Delfcroft | TL351150 |
| Ware, Chestnut Ave, garden pond | TL369152 |
| Ware, Elder Road, wild area | TL369153 |

| | |
|---|---|
| Ware, garden away from water | TL356138 |
| Wareside NE Dismantled railway | TL405158 |
| Warren, Colney Heath Common | TL201059 |
| Water Hall Quarry | TL298097 |
| Water Hall quarry, temporary wet flash/pond | TL298097 |
| Waterford Pit LNR | TL317153 |
| Waterford Pit North | TL317153 |
| Waterford Pit North, small pond | TL317151 |
| Waterford Pit South | TL318147 |
| Waterford Pit South East | TL320145 |
| Waterford Pit, North, large pond | TL317152 |
| Watery Grove, Norton Green | TL232229 |
| Watery Grove/Cannocks Wood | TL228228 |
| Watford Cheslyn Gardens pond | TQ096987 |
| Watford Link Road Pit | TQ117972 |
| Watford Louvain Way pond | TL108013 |
| Watford north Harebreaks Wood NR | TQ102992 |
| Watkins Hall Farm | TL292185 |
| Watton at Stone Scout hut pond | TL301195 |
| Watton at Stone, garden | TL304195 |
| Well End pond, near High Canons, Borehamwood | TQ204987 |
| Wellpond Green Balsams wheel ruts | TL261308 |
| Welwyn Garden City Tilbe House Pond | TL256117 |
| Welwyn Garden City, Handside Lane garden pond | TL228121 |
| Westland Green Caley Wood | TL423214 |
| Westmill Green field pond | TL348266 |
| Weston ditch near Bushwood | TL263312 |
| Weston drying wood edge pond | TL267298 |
| Weston Green End field pond | TL261308 |
| Weston Hills, Baldock | TL252322 |
| Weston meadows pond | TL265300 |
| Weston nr Church | TL266297 |
| Weston NW field pond S of Green Grove | TL262313 |
| Weston Old Vicarage pond | TL266301 |
| Weston Park, Warrens Green N of Stevenage | TL262295 |
| Weston village pond | TL258301 |
| Weston Wheelers Plat paddock pond | TL258303 |
| Weston, Hatch Lane | TL254304 |
| Wheathampstead Education Centre & fields | TL174132 |
| Wheathampstead St Helens School Pond | TL177139 |
| Wheathampstead, Field | TL180140 |
| Wheathampstead, garden pond | TL176135 |
| Whempstead, Chapel Farm, South east pond | TL314214 |
| Whempstead, garden ponds | TL321207 |
| Whempstead, Loefield Grove | TL308214 |
| Whempstead, Loefield Grove Pond 2 | TL306213 |
| Whempstead, Loefield Grove, Gregory's Farm, garden pond | TL304213 |
| Whempstead, pond North of Loefield Grove | TL308216 |
| Whempstead, pond South west of Loefield Grove | TL305214 |
| Whempstead, pond, north east of Chapel Farm | TL316215 |
| White Hill and Frythe ponds Welwyn | TL225150 |
| White House sluice stream Kingsmead | TL349139 |
| Whitehill Golf Club south of Dane End | TL341208 |
| Whomerley Wood pond, Stevenage | TL248238 |
| Wild Farm ponds Radlett | TL176011 |
| Wilkins Green Lane, Nast Hyde | TL203077 |
| Willian Roxley Court | TL227298 |

| | | | |
|---|---|---|---|
| Willian Village Pond | TL224306 | Woolmer Green village pond | TL254186 |
| Willian, Manor Farm Pond | TL223306 | Wormley Wood spring fed pond | TL322064 |
| Wilstone Gudgeon stream above GUC | SP899142 | Wormley Wood, Derry's Wood | TL323056 |
| Windridge Farm pond SW of St Albans | TL124057 | Wormley Wood, Derry's Wood Pond 1 | TL317052 |
| Wisbridge Farm | TL372363 | Wormley Wood, Derry's Wood Pond 2 | TL316055 |
| Wood End east Rush Green | TL338251 | Wormley Wood, Derry's Wood Pond 3 | TL317056 |
| Wood End west Lords Wood | TL315254 | Wormley wood, Derry's Wood Pond 4 | TL316058 |
| Woodhall Park ditch WGC | TL239120 | Wrotham Park East | TQ251993 |
| Woodhall Park, Broadwater | TL310189 | Wyddial Hall pond | TL373317 |
| Woodhill House pond Kentish Lane | TL266058 | Wyddialbury Farm field pond | TL377314 |
| Woodrow Farm | SP941093 | Wynnels Grove | TL412357 |

# Appendix C: Sources and references

For historical completeness these include obituaries of observers who made significant contributions to the study of Odonata in Hertfordshire.

*Trans HNHS* – Transactions of the Hertfordshire Natural History Society

*Brachytron* – Brachytron, Newsletter of the Hertfordshire Dragonfly Group

*J BDS* – Journal of the British Dragonfly Society

Allingham, E G (1924). *A Romance of the Rostrums. A Record of Steven's Rooms.* Witherby, London.

Askew, R R (1988). *The Dragonflies of Europe.* Harley Books, Colchester.

Attlee, H G (1935). Dragonflies in 1934. *The Entomologist* 68: 278-282.

Bath, W H (1890). *Illustrated Handbook of British Dragonflies.* Naturalists' Publishing, Birmingham.

Benson, R B (1945). Bertram Lloyd - 1881-1944. *Trans HNHS* 22: 57-59.

Benson, R B (1965). In Memorium: Mrs Sylvia Nelly Lloyd. *Trans HNHS* 26: 49.

Benton, E (1988). *The Dragonflies of Essex.* The Essex Field Club, London.

Benton, Ted & Dobson, J (2007). *The Dragonflies of Essex.* The Essex Field Club/ Lopinga Books.

British Dragonfly Society. (1996). Instructions to authors. *J BDS* 12(2). This item lists the recommended scientific (Latin) and English names adopted for the Hertfordshire records.

British Naturalists' Association. (1958-1993). *Bulletins of the Hertfordshire & Middlesex and* (latterly) *Hertfordshire Branch.*

Brooks, S J (1988a). Exotic dragonflies in North London. *J BDS* 4(1): 9-12.

Brooks, S J (1988b). Book Review. The Dragonflies of Europe, by R R Askew. *J BDS* 4(2): 46-48.

Brooks, S J (1989). The Dragonflies (*Odonata*) of London: the Current Status. *The London Naturalist* 68: 109-131.

Brown, E S (1945). *Aeshna mixta* Latr in East Hertfordshire. *Trans HNHS.* 22: 109-110.

Brown, E S (1949). Field Meeting, Saturday 27th September (1947) at Colney Heath Gravel Pits. *Trans HNHS* 23: 29-30.

Chalmers-Hunt, J M (1976). *Natural History Auctions. 1700-1972.* Sotheby Parke Bernet, London.

Cham, S A (1991). The Scarce Blue-tailed Damselfly, *Ischnura pumilio* (Charpentier): its habitat preferences in south-east England. *J BDS* 7(1): 18-25.

Cham, S A (1993). Further observations on generation time and maturation of *Ischnura pumilio* with notes on the use of a mark-recapture programme. *J BDS* 9 (2): 40-46.

Cham, S A (1996). The Scarce Blue-tailed Damselfly – the conservation of a wandering opportunist. *British Wildlife* 7: 220-225.

Cham, S A (2004). The Amazing Spread of the Small Red-eyed Damselfly across Britain. *Brachytron*. 10: 1-3.

Corbet, P S (1962). *A Biology of Dragonflies*. Witherby, London.

Corbet, P S, Longfield, C & Moore, N W (1960). *Dragonflies*. Collins, London.

Evans, W F (1845). *British Libellulinae: or Dragon Flies*. Printed for private circulation by J C Bridgewater, London.

Fraser, F C (1956). *Odonata. Handbook. Identification of British Insects 1*. Royal Ent Soc, London.

Gladwin, T W (1983). *Report on Dragonflies recorded in Hertfordshire in the years 1976 to 1983*. (Distributed privately.)

Gladwin, T W (1988a). *An Outline Ecological Evaluation of the Upper Colne Valley in Hertfordshire*. Hertfordshire County Council, Hertford.

Gladwin, T W (1994). Report for Dragonflies, 1994. *Trans HNHS* 32: 215.

Gladwin, T W (1996). The Hairy Dragonfly *Brachytron pratense* in Hertfordshire in 1992 and 1995. *Trans HNHS* 32: 433.

Gladwin, T W (1996). *Immigrant Dragonflies of the Genus Sympetrum in Hertfordshire in 1995 and 1996*. (This paper was 'missed' from the printing of *Trans HNHS* and distributed separately to record providers.)

Gladwin, T W (1997a). Report for Dragonflies for 1995 and 1996. *Trans HNHS* 33: 25-27.

Gladwin, T W (1997b). A review of the species of Dragonflies *Odonata* recorded as having been observed in Hertfordshire. *Trans HNHS* 33(1): 56-61.

Gladwin, T W (1997c). The error in treating the Green Emerald Damselfly *Lestes viridis* (Vander Linden) as a British species. *J BDS* 13(1): 29-30.

Gladwin, T W (1998b). The Dragonflies of Amwell Quarry Wildlife Reserve, 1990-July,1998. *Amwell Quarry Wildlife Reserve: Seventh Annual Report 1990-1997*. St Albans Sand & Gravel Co Ltd, Cheshunt.

Gladwin, T W (1999). The Dragonflies of the Panshanger Park. *The Ecology of the Panshanger Park, Hertfordshire*. Lafarge Redland Aggregates, 60-61.

Gladwin, T W (2000a). The Hairy Dragonfly (*Brachytron pratense*) continues its expansion in South East Herts. *Brachytron* 1: 3-4.

Gladwin, T W (2000b). Could the White-legged Damselfly (*Platycnemis pennipes*) be lost as a Hertfordshire species? *Brachytron* 1: 4.

Gladwin, T W, James, T J & White, G J (1984). *Amwell Quarry First Report 1984*. St Albans Sand & Gravel Co Ltd, Cheshunt

Gladwin, T W, James, T J & White, G J (1986). *Amwell Quarry Second Report 1985*. St Albans Sand & Gravel Co Ltd, Cheshunt.

Gladwin, T W, James, T J & White, G J (1987). *Amwell Quarry Third Report 1986*. St Albans Sand & Gravel Co Ltd, Cheshunt.

Gladwin, T W, James, T J & White, G J (1988). *Amwell Quarry Fourth Report 1987*. St Albans Sand & Gravel Co Ltd, Cheshunt.

Gladwin, T W, James, T J & White, G J (1989). *Amwell Quarry Fifth Report 1988*. St Albans Sand & Gravel Co Ltd, Cheshunt.

Gladwin, T W, James, T J & White, G J (1990). *Amwell Quarry Sixth Report 1989*. St Albans Sand & Gravel Co Ltd, Cheshunt.

Gladwin, T W and Shepperson, C (2002). Report on Dragonflies (*Odonata*) 1997-1999. *Trans HNHS* 34: 12-14.

Green, P (1987). *The South Hertfordshire Records Centre Aquatic Survey - 1987; Report A - Upper Colne Valley Gravel Pits*.

Gregory, P H (1975). The Natural History of the Hertfordshire Natural History Society. *Trans HNHS* 27: 336-347.

Griffiths, R J (1942). Field Meeting, Saturday 28th June (1941) in Cassiobury Park and Whippendell Woods. *Trans HNHS* 21: 51.

Hammond, C O (2nd Ed 1983). *The Dragonflies of Great Britain and Ireland*. Harley Books, Colchester.

Harris, M A (1998). The Status of Odonata at Rye Meads 1996. *14th Report of the Rye Meads Ringing Group*: 60-65.

Hayward, H H S (1968) In Memoriam, S B Hodgson. *Trans HNHS* 26: 218. S B Hodgson's diaries are in the North Hertfordshire museum.

Hayward, H H S & M G (1945). Dragonflies of the Lea Canal. *Trans HNHS* 22: 89-90.

Herbert, C (1994). *Dragonflies and Damselflies of the London Borough of Barnet*. HMWT, St. Albans.

Hertfordshire Biological Records Centre (1997-8). *Reports on the Hertfordshire Habitat Survey Project* (10 vols). Hertfordshire County Council, Hertford

Hertfordshire Dragonfly Group. (2000-04). *Brachytron* Issues 1-10.

Hine, R L (1934). *The Natural History of the Hitchin Region*. Hitchin & District Regional Survey Association, Hitchin. The section on Odonata is a complete reproduction of Palmer (1930).

Hodgson, S B (1959). West Hertfordshire Dragonflies. *Trans HNHS* 25: 68-72.

Hodgson, S B (1960a). Dragonflies Preying on Butterflies. *Trans HNHS* 25: 108.

Hodgson, S B (1960b). *Sympetrum sanguineum* in Hertfordshire. *Trans HNHS* 25: 108-109.

Hodgson, S B (1961). Seasonal Regulation in Dragonflies. *Trans HNHS* 25: 167-168.

Hodgson, S B (1962). Notes on the Emperor Dragonfly. *Trans HNHS* 25: 205-206.

Hopkinson, J (Editor 1911). St Albans and its Neighbourhood. *Trans HNHS* 14: 209-254. The section on Odonata was contributed by A E Gibbs.

James, T J (1989a). Old Parkbury Gravel Pits for Entomology, 26th July 1986. *Trans HNHS* 30: 162.

James, T J (1989b). Therfield and Nuthampstead for Birds. 5th October 1986. *Trans HNHS* 30: 164.

Jane, F W (1946). The Natural History of Hertfordshire. *Trans HNHS* 22: 142-159.

Lloyd, B (1937). Dragonflies at Elstree Reservoir and District. *Trans HNHS* 20: 91-94.

Lloyd, B (1938). Dragonflies at Elstree Reservoir and District (II). *Trans HNHS* 20: 328-332.

Lloyd, B (1939). Hertfordshire Dragonflies – Corrections and a New Record. *Trans HNHS* 21: 123-124.

Lloyd, B (1941). A new emergence of the dragonfly *Coenagrion puella*. *The Entomologist* 74: 113-114.

Lloyd, B (1942). *Platycnemis pennipes* in Hertfordshire. *The Entomologist* 75: 161-162.

Lloyd, B (1944). West Hertfordshire Dragonflies. *Trans HNHS* 22: 43-47.

Lloyd, S (1948). Report on Dragonflies Observed in Hertfordshire in 1946. *Trans HNHS* 23: 21-23.

Lloyd, S (1949a). Field Meeting, Saturday 26th July (1947), at Elstree Reservoir. *Trans HNHS* 23: 28.

Lloyd, S (1949b). Field Characters of Some Dragonflies. *Trans HNHS* 23: 65-71.

Lloyd, S (1950). Field Meeting, Saturday 7th August, (1948) at Wall Hall, Aldenham. *Trans HNHS* 23: 43.

Lloyd, S (1952a). Field Meeting, Saturday 13th August (1949), at Elstree Reservoir. *Trans HNHS* 23: 57.

Lloyd, S (1952b). Notes on Dragonflies Observed in Hertfordshire in 1947-1949. *Trans HNHS* 23: 234-235.

Lloyd, S (1953). Report on Dragonflies Observed in Hertfordshire 1950-1951. *Trans HNHS* 24: 35-37.

Lloyd, S (1954). Report on Dragonflies Observed in Hertfordshire in 1952. *Trans HNHS* 24: 75-77.

Lloyd, S (1956). Report on Dragonflies Observed in Hertfordshire, 1953 and 1954. *Trans HNHS* 24: 190-191.

Lloyd, S (1957). Enemies of Dragonflies. *Trans HNHS* 24: 226-229.

Lloyd, S (1958). Report on Dragonflies Observed in Hertfordshire in 1955 and 1956. *Trans HNHS* 25: 29-32.

Lloyd, S (1959). Report on Dragonflies Observed in Hertfordshire in 1957. *Trans HNHS* 25: 66-67.

Lloyd, S (1960). Report on Dragonflies Observed in Hertfordshire in 1958. *Trans HNHS* 25: 94-95.

Lloyd, S (1961). Report on Dragonflies Observed in Hertfordshire in 1959. *Trans HNHS* 25: 164-166.

Lloyd, S (1962). Report on Dragonflies Observed in Hertfordshire in 1960. *Trans HNHS* 25: 197-199.

Lloyd, S (1963). Report on Dragonflies Observed in Hertfordshire in 1961. *Trans HNHS* 25: 245-246.

Longfield, C (1937). *The Dragonflies of the British Isles* (1st Edition). Warne, London.

Longfield, C (1949a). *The Dragonflies of the British Isles* (2nd Edition). Warne, London.

Longfield, C (1949b). The Dragonflies (Odonata) of the London Area. *The London Naturalist*. 28: 90-98.

Longfield, C (1949c). The Breeding Status of *Aeshna mixta* Latreille (Odonata) and Notes on the Evidence of Breeding in *Sympetrum flaveolum* (L.) and *S. fonscolombii* (Sélys). *J. Soc. for Brit. Ent.* 3: 84-88.

Longfield, C (1954). The British Dragonflies (Odonata) in 1952 and 1953. *The Entomologist* 87: 87-91.

Looker, S J (1960). *Bertram Lloyd (1891-1944)*. Published privately by S J Looker & Mrs Sylvia Lloyd, Aylesbury.

Lucas, W J (1900). *British Dragonflies (Odonata)*. Upcott Gill, London.

Lucas, W J (1904). Dragonflies in 1902 and 1903. *The Entomologist* 37: 29-34.

McGeeney, A (1986). *A Complete Guide to British Dragonflies*. Jonathan Cape, London.

Marshall, I (Revised Edition 1987). *Report of the Hertfordshire Pond Survey, 1986*. Hertfordshire County Council, Hertford.

Merritt, R, Moore, N W & Eversham, B C (1996). *Atlas of the Dragonflies of Britain and Ireland*. HMSO, London.

Middleton, A (2001). Discovery of the Small Red-eyed Damselfly in the Lea Valley. *Brachytron*. 3: 4-5.

Murray, S H (1993). The Dragonflies of Hilfield Park Reservoir: 1992. *Hilfield Park Reservoir Bird Report for 1992*. 17-18.

Murray, S H (1994). The Dragonflies of Hilfield Park Reservoir: 1993. *Hilfield Park Reservoir Bird Report for 1993*. 19.

Murray, S H (2004). Blue Female Broad-bodied Chaser. *Brachytron*. 9: 8.

Myer, D & H (1976). In Memoriam: Ray Palmer, F Z S (1896-1975). *Trans HNHS* 27: 321-322.

Newton, R (1975). Butterflies and Dragonflies recorded in the Lea Valley. *Lea Valley Project Group Bird Report 1974*.

O'Hara, D P (1952). General Entomological Report. *Haileybury and Imperial Service College Nat Hist Soc Annual Report for 1951: 11-12*.

Page, W (Editor 1902). *The Victoria History of the Counties of England: Hertfordshire*.

Palmer, R (1930). Dragonflies Observed in Hertfordshire. *Trans HNHS* 19: 48-50. This paper is reproduced in Hine (1934).

Palmer, R (1940). Hertfordshire Dragonflies. *Trans HNHS* 21: 167-172.

Palmer, R (undated). *List of specimens of dragonflies in the Hertfordshire County Museum, St Albans* (unpublished).

Parr, A J (1996). Dragonfly movement and migration in Britain and Ireland. *J BDS* 12(2): 33-50.

Parr, A J (1997a). Migrant and dispersive dragonflies in Britain during 1996. *J BDS* 13(2): 41-47.

Parr, A J (1997b). The 1996 Red-veined Darter *Sympetrum fonscolombii* (Sélys,) influx into Britain. *Atropos* 2: 44-46.

Pinniger, E B (1937). Notes on Dragonflies, 1936. *London Naturalist* 16: 54-56. Correspondence confirms that the records of *Aeshna cyanea, A. grandis* and *Sympetrum striolatum* for September 18th 1936 were obtained in Hertfordshire.

Pittman, S (1996). Migrant species of *Sympetrum* in Norfolk, 1995. *J BDS* 12(1): 1.

Reynolds, A (2002). Black Darter at Hertford Heath. *Brachytron*. 6: 4-5.

Reynolds, A. (2003a). Hairy Dragonfly at Kings Meads. *Brachytron*. 8: 2.

Reynolds, A (2003b). The First Keeled Skimmer for Hertfordshire. *Brachytron*. 8: 9.

Reynolds, A (2003c). Flight Seasons of the Common and Ruddy Darters. *Brachytron*. 8: 9-11.

Sage, B L (1961). The Supposed Occurrence of the Dragonfly *Lestes viridis* Van der Linden in Hertfordshire. *Trans HNHS* 25: 167.

Sage, B L (1964). Report on Dragonflies Recorded in Hertfordshire in 1962 and 1963. *Trans HNHS* 26: 34-36.

Sage, B L (1966). Report on Dragonflies Recorded in Hertfordshire in 1964 and 1965. *Trans HNHS* 26: 143-146.

Sage, B L (1968). Report on Dragonflies Recorded in Hertfordshire in 1966 and 1967. *Trans HNHS* 26: 260-262.

Sage, B L (1970). Report on Dragonflies in Hertfordshire in 1968 and 1969. *Trans HNHS* 27: 74-77.

Sage, B L (1973). Report on Dragonflies in Hertfordshire in 1970, 1971 and 1972. *Trans HNHS* 27: 232-236.

Sage, B L (1975). Report on Dragonflies in Hertfordshire in 1973, 1974 and 1975. *Trans HNHS* 27: 331-335.

Sage B L (1998). A Hertfordshire record of the Small Red Damselfly *Ceriagrion tenellum* (Villers). *J BDS* 14(2): 60.

Sawford, B (1990). *Wild Flower Habitats of Hertfordshire*. Castlemead, Ware.

Shepperson, C (1997). Some Dragonfly Observations: Summer 1996. *HNHS Newsletter*. July 1997: 2-3. (With comments from Revd Tom Gladwin).

Shepperson, C (1998). *A Review of Dragonflies and Damselflies in Hertfordshire 1992-1998*. Published privately and distributed by the author.

Shepperson, C (2000). *A Review of Dragonflies and Damselflies in Hertfordshire 1999*. Published privately and distributed by the author.

Shepperson, C (2000a). The Hairy Dragonfly – The Expansion Continues. *Brachytron* 2: 7-8.

Shepperson, C (2000b). The Fortunes of the White-legged Damselfly. *Brachytron* 2: 9.

Shepperson, C (2001a). The Hairy Dragonfly in Herts 2001: A Year of Consolidation. *Brachytron* 4: 5-6.

Shepperson, C (2001b). The White-legged Damselfly; an interesting season. *Brachytron* 4: 6-7.

Shepperson, C (2002). The White-legged Damselfly: A New Colony Discovered. *Brachytron* 6: 9-10.

Shepperson, C (2003a). White-legged Damselflies Move North. *Brachytron* 8: 5.

Shepperson, C (2003b). Small Red-eyed Damselflies on the move in Herts. *Brachytron* 8: 6-9.

Shepperson, C (2004). The Hairy Dragonfly (*Brachytron pratense*): Is it firmly established in Hertfordshire? *Brachytron* 9: 6-7.

Shepperson, C & Anderson, D (2004). Recent Observations of egg laying away from water by Herts. Dragonfly Group Members. *Brachytron* 10: 4-7.

Shirley, D (Editor 1978). *Hertfordshire – a guide to the countryside*. Egon Publishers, Letchworth.

Silsby, J & Ward-Smith, J (1997). The influx of *Sympetrum flaveolum* (L) during the summer of 1995. *J BDS* 13(1): 14-22.

Speyer, E R (1910). Notes on Odonata observed in Great Britain during the Summer of 1908. *The Entomologist* 43: 13-18.

Speyer, E R (1911). Notes on Odonata Observed in Great Britain during the Summers of 1909 and 1910. *The Entomologist*. 44: 283-286.

Speyer, E R (1949). An occurence of *Ischnura pumilio* Charp (Odonata) in Hertfordshire. *Jnl. Soc for Brit Ent* 3: 45.

Stephens, J F (1835). *Illustrations of British Entomology; or a Synopsis of Indigenous Insects*. Vol.VI. Baldwin and Cradock, London.

Wainwright, E D (Editor 1926). *Fauna and Flora of Haileybury*. (Third Issue). Stephen Austin, Hertford. Includes the list of dragonflies compiled by D G Sevastopoulo, in 1920.

Ward, R (2003). *London's New River*. Historical Publications, London.

Ward-Smith, J (1997). Records of *Sympetrum fonscolombii* (Says) and *Sympetrum vulgatum* (L) for the summer of 1995. *J BDS* 13(2): 59-60.

White, G J (1986). *Changes in the Dragonfly Populations of the Lea Valley*. Unpublished paper 13pp.

White, G J (2002). The first Small Red-eyed Damselfly for Hertfordshire. *Brachytron* 6: 3.

Winbold, G E (1949). Report on Odonata. *Haileybury and Imperial Service College Nat Hist Soc Annual Report for 1949* 15-17.

Winbold, G E (1950). Report on Odonata. *Haileybury and Imperial Service College Nat Hist Soc Annual Report for 1950*: 18.

# Index